Reprints of Economic Classics

LABOR THEORY OF VALUE

HISTORY AND CRITICISM

OF THE

LABOR THEORY OF VALUE

IN ENGLISH POLITICAL ECONOMY

BY

ALBERT C. WHITAKER

[1904]

REPRINTS OF ECONOMIC CLASSICS

AUGUSTUS M. KELLEY · PUBLISHERS
NEW YORK 1968

First Edition 1904

(New York: Columbia University, 1904)

Reprinted 1968 by
AUGUSTUS M. KELLEY · PUBLISHERS
New York New York 10010

Library of Congress Catalogue Card Number

66-21702

Printed in the United States of America
by Sentry Press, New York, N. Y. 10019

HISTORY AND CRITICISM

OF THE

LABOR THEORY OF VALUE

IN ENGLISH POLITICAL ECONOMY

BY

ALBERT C. WHITAKER, A. B.,

Sometime University Fellow in Economics, Columbia University ;
Instructor in Economics, Leland Stanford Junior University

SUBMITTED IN PARTIAL FULFILMENT OF THE REQUIREMENTS
FOR THE DEGREE OF DOCTOR OF PHILOSOPHY
IN THE
FACULTY OF POLITICAL SCIENCE,
COLUMBIA UNIVERSITY

Columbia University
1904

CONTENTS

CHAPTER XI

THE ULTIMATE RELATION OF COST TO VALUE

ERRATA.

P. 89. 3d line from bottom. Insert " in " before " different times."

P. 92. 6th and 7th lines from top. For " intrinsic " read " extrinsic."

CHAPTER I

GENERAL OUTLINES OF THE HISTORY OF THE LABOR THEORY OF VALUE

1. THE following history of the labor theory of value begins with Adam Smith, not because it is supposed that Political Economy was born with the *Wealth of Nations,* but because no other work written affords so convenient a starting-point to the historian who has no desire to press his investigations into regions too remote from modern interests.

After Adam Smith, the writers to be considered are Ricardo and Malthus, McCulloch, James Mill and Torrens, Senior, John Stuart Mill, and Cairnes. In the next great treatise after that of Cairnes, the *Principles of Economics* of Marshall, there is nothing left of the labor theory of value, except a note at the end of a chapter on the general theory of the equilibrium of supply and demand.[1] This note, "On Ricardo's Theory of Value," endeavors to state the ultimate relations of cost, utility and value in such a manner that Ricardo's explanation of value is made to appear as a statement true as far as it goes, which errs only in being incomplete, and which is completed, not refuted, by the utility theory. This view will be taken up in the last chapter of the present essay. But no separate chapter is devoted to Professor Marshall's work, because, as a matter of fact, the Ricardian labor theory finds no place in the text of his *Principles.* From Smith to Cairnes, the list of writers given

---

[1] Chap. xiv of book v, 4th ed., 1898, pp. 554–570.

above was selected as well calculated to exhibit the general line of development of English political economy. No attempt has been made to discover writers outside of this list, although it is not denied that such writers may not at present receive due credit for their influence upon the development of economic theory. Making no attempt at what might be called a discursive or *extensive* study of the field, this history will be confined to an *intensive* study of the chief writers. If it be found that certain of the above list of writers contributed nothing but error to the theory of value—and such is the case with three of them—even such a conclusion is deemed to be of historical value.

2. With the limits of our field thus defined, attention should first be called to a fairly prevalent, but mistaken, impression regarding the so-called classical labor theory of value. It is frequently assumed that this theory of value was a simple and absolute dictum, supported in substantial unanimity by a considerable body of writers, called collectively " the classical school." There is, no doubt, sufficient resemblance among these writers in their general tendencies of thought to justify the term " classical school;" but with respect to their views on the central problem of value, it is their differences of opinion that at present need emphasis, just as it is these differences which take the modern reader by surprise when he first undertakes a detailed study of their writings. Instead of finding the minds of the early English economists dominated by a single labor theory, having the merit of great directness and simplicity, the historian of the theory is confronted with an appalling jumble of ideas on the relation of labor to value. Ricardo, it is true, defended the simple thesis that the exchange value of a commodity is governed by its cost of production in labor, but it is sometimes forgotten that he hedged this doctrine about with several important qualifications and conditions. Fur-

thermore, there was not a contemporary or subsequent writer who did not differ from Ricardo in important points of theory. Taking Smith, Malthus, Ricardo, McCulloch, Torrens, and James Mill together, we find labor sometimes conceived of as *disutility cost,* at other times as *productive power,* without any recognition of the distinction between these concepts. Yet this distinction may be of great importance in certain propositions of theory. We find McCulloch at one time claiming that the value-determining labor employed in the production of a commodity includes the operations of machines and inanimate objects, which are " philosophically just as truly labor as human exertions." Torrens maintained that value is governed by cost of production in " accumulated " labor, and James Mill held interest on capital to be really wages of labor, an absurd thought absolutely foreign to Ricardo's theory. In addition to the *labor-cost regulator* of value, there was the *labor-command measure* of value, the measure of the value [1] of a good for all times and places, alleged to be afforded by the amount of labor which could be commanded by it or had in exchange for it. The principal defender of this measure, Malthus, did not believe in the labor-cost regulator. It was asserted that the " value of labor " is the same in all times and places. When this value is inadvertently identified with *exchange value,* which must, of course, be measured by the commodity wages of labor, some highly interesting arguments are necessitated to show that real wages are in some sense or other the same in all times and places, in spite of the fact that, as commonly understood, they are by no means the same. We find a " corn measure " of value first proposed as a convenient index to the true labor measure. But,

---

[1] Value was in this connection used in another sense than pure exchange value, but the difference of significance was never satisfactorily explained.

strange to say, later we run upon a proposal to take an
" arithmetic mean between corn and labor " (*i. e.,* between
their prices) as the " least defective measure " of " intrinsic
value in exchange." *Cost of production* was used without
any distinguishing adjectives to indicate concepts so distinct
as entrepreneur's cost and labor cost (presumably " disutility cost "). In consequence there arose a dispute, which
was at the time nearly unintelligible, as to whether or not
profits (*i. e.,* interest on capital) are a part of cost of production.

3. In the confusion, a few main lines of thought can be dis-
cerned. There is a theory of value *regulation,* and there is
a theory of value *measurement,* which is, as Malthus and
others pointed out, a distinct thing from value regulation.
The classical theory of value *regulation* was composed of
two separate accounts. That is, these two accounts were
of distinct origin and nature, and should have been kept
distinct. Instead of this they were more or less fused and
the relation between them was always clouded. To this fact
is due the great difficulty all must experience in reaching a
complete understanding of the classical theory. Though it
is for this reason very necessary to give the accounts separate names, it seems impossible to find unobjectionable terms.
Professor von Wieser, from whom I have taken the idea
that the confusion between these two accounts is the key to
the history of the labor theory of value, distinguishes them
by the terms " philosophical " and " empirical." [1]

---

[1] *Natural Value,* edited by Wm. Smart (London, 1893), pp. xxvii-
xxix. Von Wieser gives but three pages of the preface of *Natural
Value* to the writings of Adam Smith and Ricardo on value. But in
this brief though profound passage, he has not only suggested what I
believe to be the true interpretation of the theories of Smith and Ricardo, but he has also made the greatest single contribution to our
understanding of the subsequent course of English thought on the
subject.

Adopting these names, in default of better, the "philosophical" account is the answer of the fathers of modern political economy to the general riddle of value, the riddle of its ultimate nature, or essence. At first blush it would seem that things must derive their value from their usefulness. But almost immediately the mind turns to the fact, which has since "classical" days become such a time-honored illustration, that bread is "more useful" than gold, but much less valuable. The usefulness of bread, as it is here understood, is its general or characteristic usefulness, its usefulness as a class of things, its power to preserve our health and strength. Meditating upon the importance of the entire class of utilities represented by bread, one is led to ignore the question whether the specific utility of a particular piece of bread, in the given circumstances of the supply of bread, is not less than the specific usefulness of a particular piece of gold for purposes of ornament, in the given circumstances of the supply of gold. This is the line of inquiry which leads to the utility theory. But having passed the place where this road branches off, the earlier speculation on value reached the conclusion that things possessing utility have their values determined by their cost in labor. This answer to the riddle seems foreordained, when once Adam Smith's "value in use" is adopted as the sole conception of utility. Elaboration and illustration of this philosophy always leads to primitive and "natural" society, where the hunter and fisherman, rent-free and equal, exchange the products of their labor as measured in days. When, however, the attention turns to the market-price of goods in the actual world, it is observed as a matter of business experience, in contrast with speculation with regard to the essence of things, that the exchange value of commodities tends to equal the sum of the wages of labor, the

" profits " of stock, and the rent of land [1] which must be paid to obtain their production. This is the " empirical " account. The principle discovered is that now known as the law of entrepreneur's costs.[2]

The central idea in the " philosophical " account is that labor-cost is the essence of value. It appeals primarily to the reader's introspective judgment for confirmation. The primitive state of society by which it is illustrated is quite imaginary. The " empirical " account is an outwardly observed tendency of market competition. In the progress of the thought of English economists upon value, the " philosophical " labor-cost account becomes more and more attenuate, until in the *Principles* of Professor Marshall, as before observed, nothing remains of it but a note on " Ricardo's Theory of Value." Professor Marshall's general theory of the equilibrium of normal demand and supply is the classical " empirical " account enlarged and greatly improved, with some of the more general laws of the newer utility theory incorporated into the whole to serve as the ultimate principles of demand. While the " philosophical " account was fading away, the " empirical " account was becoming virtually the whole theory of value. Strange to say, Ricardo contributed very little to the advancement of the empirical account as such. The direct line of descent of this doctrine is traceable from Smith's *Wealth of Nations,* through the *Principles* of Malthus and J. S. Mill, to Marshall. Neither Ricardo nor Cairnes can be considered to stand in the line.[3]

[1] Rent of land was excluded by Ricardo, but included by Smith and Malthus, and also by J. B. Say.

[2] The Austrian writers are accustomed to call this the "empirical law of costs."

[3] The detailed history given in the following chapters will, it is believed, substantiate this view. The development of the law of entrepreneur's costs will be traced only so far as is necessary in order to under-

Adam Smith and Malthus considered ground-rent to be a " component part " of entrepreneur's cost (not that they employed the term entrepreneur's cost), co-ordinate with wages and " profits of stock."   Ricardo never stated a law of entrepreneur's cost plainly, formally, as such, though he gave it an obscure recognition as a source of difficulty to the pure labor theory of value.   But he influenced its form profoundly, for when the doctrine passed into the hands of J. S. Mill, the latter removed the rent of land from among the elements of cost, leaving wages and interest.[1]

While many points of detail will appear in the following pages, it will be found necessary to trace the relations of the two great accounts of value, the " philosophical " and the " empirical," in the writings of every economist hereafter considered.

stand the history of the labor theory, but it is indispensable to follow the general lines of its progress if we are to perceive the "setting" of the labor theory.

[1] Mill granted certain exceptions to the proposition that rent cannot "enter into price," but placed no emphasis upon them.

CHAPTER II

1. THERE is a veritable multiplicity of explanations of value in the *Wealth of Nations,* which makes a history of Adam Smith's views on this subject extremely difficult writing. Many a wise or philosophical sort of observation may be correct in a general way, or largely true, and yet not be precisely true. Perhaps the greater part of what Adam Smith has said on the nature of value consists of reflections of this kind, and the student of his text can never be certain that he really planned to describe the laws of value with that precision which modern theory at least hopes to attain. Still there are some exact theorems laid down. The language in which these are expressed is uniformly flowing and makes good reading; but it seems to be more an eloquent appeal against the shallow mercantilist view of wealth, than an attempt at a painstaking analysis of the facts of value. The following thoroughly typical passage from the chapter, " Of the Real and Nominal Price of Commodities, or of their Price in Labor and their Price in Money," is truly a call to people to look away from money as the sole measure of wealth and regard the real source of wealth. But in spite of this it happens to end in a precise proposition or theory of value:

" Wealth, as Mr. Hobbes says, is power. But the person who either acquires, or succeeds to a great fortune, does not

16 [274

necessarily acquire or succeed to any political power, either civil or military. * * * * The power which that posses-sion immediately and directly conveys to him, is the power of purchasing, a certain command over all the labour, or over all the produce of labour which is then in the market. His fortune is greater or less, precisely in proportion to the extent of, his power; or to the quantity either of other men's labour, or, what is the same thing, of the produce of other men's labour, which it enables him to purchase or command. The exchangeable value of everything must always be precisely equal to the extent of this power which it conveys to its owner." [1]

From which Adam Smith concludes that labor is " the real measure of the exchangeable value of all commodities." The exact meaning of the conclusion, it must be observed, is not plain. If " exchangeable value " meant mere ex-change value in the modern sense—the power of a good to exchange for some quantity of another good objectively measured in weight, volume, or length—then money would afford a measure of this value quite as reliable as labor and far more convenient. What is intended by " exchangeable value " is a question we may approach later, but whatever exact meaning we take for this term, we find that the series of general observations preceding the conclusion does not prove this conclusion as a precise proposition. This pas-sage is typical of the chapter. Painstaking study of Smith's theory or theories of value is also made difficult by occa-sional lapses into very loose terminology. For an instance, we find the sentence, " equal quantities of labor, at all times and places, may be said to be of equal value to the laborer." [2]

[1] *Wealth of Nations*, 2d Thorold Rogers ed., 1880, pp. 31-2. All sub-sequent page references are to this edition, volume 1.

[2] P. 34.

The context shows that, in all probability, value here means *disutility*.[1]

The several different minor theories of value given by Adam Smith are not woven into a whole by him. The student of his views approaches his great work with a respect that amounts to awe, and it takes time to force himself to the conclusion that there is a part of the *Wealth of Nations* which, though profoundly suggestive, is not entirely consistent. The attempt, instinctively made by the commentator, to find a hidden consistency behind the various incompatible utterances, to discover a hypothesis upon which the contradictions may be declared apparent only, is, according to the belief of the writer, fore-doomed to complete failure.

Within the plurality of explanations of value two main divisions are discernible, the first contained in Chapter V, and the second in Chapters VI and VII of Book I.[2] These are the "philosophical" and the "empirical" accounts distinguished in the first chapter of this essay. The first of these is in its place stated in general terms, as if unconditionally true, but when the empirical account is reached, a considerable part of what had been said previously is restricted to "that early and rude state of society which precedes both the accumulation of stock and the appropriation of land."[3] For this reason what has been called the "phil-

[1] Referring to the words just quoted, Mr. Ingram says: "This sentence, which on close examination will be found to have no definite intelligible sense, affords a good example of the way in which metaphysical modes of thought obscure economic ideas." *History of Political Economy*, p. 94, note.

[2] Chap. v. "Of the Real and Nominal Price of Commodities, or of their Price in Labour and their Price in Money." Chap. vi. "Of the Component Parts of the Price of Commodities." Chap. vii. "Of the Natural and Market Price of Commodities."

[3] P. 49. At the same time many important assertions in the "philosophical account" are not restricted to primitive conditions.

osophical," may, in the case of Adam Smith, also be called
the " primitive " account of value.

2. Preparatory to taking up the philosophical account, a
few words on the use of the terms labor and value are per-
tinent.   The word *labor,* now as formerly, denotes really
two distinct, though related, things.   One is the *productive
power* of human beings.   For instance, labor and natural
agents are called factors in production, or it is said that the
entrepreneur purchases labor.   The other is the *disutility*
or *discomfort* endured by men in the course of production,
as in the sentence: " This article has cost me much labor."[1]
Productive power may be accompanied by no disutility, or
by moderate or high disutility, according to circumstances.
Labor is used in both senses by Adam Smith.   As for the
word *value,* Smith explains at the outset that the term has
two meanings, " value in use " and " value in exchange,"
and restricts his investigations to the principles of the
" exchangeable value."   This is defined as the " power of
purchasing other goods " which an object " conveys " to its
owner.[2]   But Adam Smith does not explain nor appear to
realize that he uses the term " exchangeable value " in two
senses.   When he asserts that the " real worth " of anything to a man " is the toil and trouble which it can save
himself, and which it can impose on other people," and that
therefore labor is the real measure of the " exchangeable
value of all commodities;" " exchangeable value " means
something other than mere purchasing power.   Writing

---

[1] It is true that an article's cost in labor may instead mean its cost in
productive power. The cost in this case is at bottom the utility of some
other article which might have been created by this productive power
had it not been employed in making the first article. In the same sense
we speak of a thing as costing money.

[2] P. 29, in chap. iv.

nearly a century later, Menger said that value is that significance (*Bedeutung*) which a good attains in our estimation when we feel the satisfaction of some want to be *conditioned* upon it. This is "*esteem* value," or value as
Bedeutung. Smith's concept, of value as " real worth,"
which he has miscalled " exchangeable " value, is something analogous to this. But Smith finds the significance
in labor instead of in satisfaction.[1]

3. Turning now directly to the "philosophical" account,
we find the multiplicity of Adam Smith's explanations of
value illustrated once more by the fact that within this
chapter he suggests two distinct labor standards. One is
given as a *regulator* of value, a something which quantita-
tively governs value. The other is merely a *measure* of
value. There is no adequate discussion of the mutual relations of the two. Both appear in the following sentence:

" What everything is worth to the man who has acquired
it, and who wants to dispose of it or exchange it for something else, is the toil and trouble which it can save to himself,
and which it can impose on other people." [2]

The " toil " saved " to himself " must be the labor cost of
reproduction, not distinguished by Smith from cost of production. The two standards are asserted separately. In
an early and rude state of society,

" the proportion between the quantities of labour necessary for
acquiring different objects seems to be the only circumstance

[1] It has been suggested by many writers that the germ of practically
every theory of value is found in the *Wealth of Nations*. That is probably true, if we except the utility theory, which associates quantity of
value with *quantity of utility*, a conception absolutely foreign to Adam
Smith's thought.

[2] P. 31.

which can afford any rule for exchanging them for one another." [1]

And

" at all times and places, that is dear * * * * which it costs much labour to acquire." [2]

And again:

" The value of any commodity to the person who possesses it [and wishes to exchange it] is equal to the quantity of labour which it enables him to purchase or command. Labour, therefore, is the real measure of the exchangeable value of all commodities." [3]

The first of these, in accordance with which it is asserted that value is governed (in the philosophical primitive conditions) by cost in labor, may be called the *labor-cost standard.* The second finds a convenient name as the *labor-command standard.*[4] The two play separate and important parts in the subsequent history of the labor theory of value. Ricardo adopted the labor-cost standard as applicable to the conditions of advanced or capitalistic society and repudiated the labor-command measure. Malthus, on the contrary, defended the latter and rejected the former.[5]

---

[1] P. 49.   [2] P. 34.   [3] P. 30.

[4] In this instance the word "standard" is used in a sense sufficiently general to include a regulator (*i. e.*, a measuring cause) and a mere measure. A standard is "1. Any measure of extent, quantity, quality or value." . . . "2. Any fact, thing or circumstance forming a basis for adjustment and regulation." *Standard Dictionary.*

[5] What Adam Smith has to say of the relation of these standards, one to the other, comes in connection with the account for advanced society, where he discards the labor-cost standard but retains the labor-command measure.

4. Since the amount of the value of a good is asserted to bear certain definite relations to the amount of labor it costs or commands, it is a very proper question to inquire how quantity of labor is measured in any particular case. Adam Smith remarks that the quantity of money for which a good can be exchanged is " a plain palpable object," but that the quantity of labor which it commands, indirectly through the use of money is " an abstract notion, which, though it can be made sufficiently intelligible, it (*sic*) is not altogether so natural and obvious." [1] He suggests, in that most excellent and familiar Smithian sentence, that the proportions in which different concrete kinds of labor exchange (or count for quantity of labor in general or in the abstract) are

" adjusted not by any accurate measure, but by the higgling and bargaining of the market, according to that sort of rough equality which, though not exact, is sufficient for carrying on the business of common life." [2]

Nevertheless there are certain principles which enable us to define quantity of labor in a general way. Time alone spent at a task does not determine the quantity of labor put forth. The different degrees of hardship endured and of ingenuity exercised in different employments must also be considered.

If we should assume for the moment that there were exact units of disutility and skill as of time, Adam Smith's theory would signify that the quantity of labor in any particular case is measured by time units weighted with units of disutility and of skill. The amount of two different kinds of labor commanded in exchange by any commodity depends upon the wages commonly earned at these kinds of labor. If a certain commodity, worth such and such a sum of money, commands in exchange one day of labor in em-

[1] P. 32.   [2] *Ibid.*

ployment A and two days in employment B, Adam Smith would be forced to assume that one day of A is the same quantity of labor as two days of B.   At bottom, then, the theory means that one day of A is the same quantity of labor as two days of B, because these two pieces of labor get the same wages.

Taking it for granted that the amount of wages paid (under competitive conditions) is a true test of the *quantity* of labor in any given concrete task, we shall find some further speculation on this question if we turn to the famous chapter upon the inequality of wages in different employments.[1] In this chapter there is a suggestion that the extra reward for skilled labor is a disguised payment for superior disutility.   The following analogy drawn between skill and a machine has been used by many later writers:

" When any expensive machine is erected, the extraordinary work to be performed by it before it is worn out, it must be expected, will replace the capital laid out upon it, with at least the ordinary profits.   A man educated at the expense of much labour and time to any of those employments which require extraordinary dexterity and skill, may be compared to one of those expensive machines.   The work which he learns to perform, it must be expected, over and above the usual wages of common labour, will replace to him the whole expense of his education, with at least the ordinary profits of an equally valuable capital.   * * *   The difference between the wages of skilled labour and those of common labour is founded upon this principle." [2]

Thus skill represents disutility incurred in its acquisition, and the surplus reward to skill is virtually reward to disutility in a form bearing analogies to interest.   This is for acquired skill.   What is to be said of inborn skill, of native

[1] Chap. x, of book i.   [2] P. 106.

superior talents? This question apparently escapes Adam Smith. Uniformly, the tacit assumption underlying his thought seems to be that of the inborn equality of powers in men. Keeping this assumption in mind, we see that Smith's view amounts to the theory that all occupations are about equally well rewarded, all things considered. Higher wages are paid only where there is more labor, ultimately in the sense of *disutility*. The *inequalities* of wages are such only in proportion to the *time* of labor.[1]

To give a mid-chapter summary of results—put together by ourselves rather than by Smith—if the exchange values of goods are to be governed by the quantity of labor which they have cost, and the " real worth " of goods is to be measured either by the quantity of labor they have cost or by that which they can command in exchange, there must be some means of defining the *quantity* of labor in different employments. Adam Smith has made this depend, in the first instance, upon time compounded with amounts of disutility and skill. But he has further suggested that the element of skill really represents a past disutility. The principal assumption involved is that all occupations are competed for by men born equal in efficiency. If he did not clearly avoid the appearance of laying down hard and fast principles, we could conclude that he meant *quantity of disutility* by quantity of labor.

5. The dictum that labor is the means of measuring the " real worth " of goods does not, I believe, necessarily in-

---

[1] In one place Smith puts forward a naive and uncritical explanation of the reward to skill, comparable to his explanation of the division of labor as due to a propensity of men to truck and barter. "If . . . one species of labour requires an uncommon degree of dexterity and inge-nuity, *the esteem which men have for such talents will naturally* give a value to their produce superior to what would be due to the time em-ployed about it." P. 49.

volve the notion that this measure can be used to compare the value of a good in A. D. 1400 with its value in 1800, or its value in China with that in England. An important part of the chapter on the real and nominal price of commodities is given over to the claim that labor furnishes an "invariable measure" of value in all times and places. Money, the most convenient measure of value in a given time and place, varies in its value in different times and places. But

"Equal quantities of labour, at all times and places, may be said to be of equal value to the labourer. In his ordinary state of health, strength and spirits, in the ordinary degree of his skill and dexterity, he must always lay down the same portion of his ease, his liberty, and his happiness. The price which he pays must always be the same, whatever may be the quantity of goods which he receives in return for it. * * * Labour alone, therefore, never varying in its own value, is alone the ultimate and real standard by which the value of all commodities can at all times and places be estimated and compared." [1]

In this passage the misuse of the word value is flagrant, but the meaning is plain. No matter what be the physical quantity of goods which a day of labor either produces or earns as wages, the value of these goods, in the sense of *significance* to human welfare, is the same, *because* they cost the same amount of disutility. The person who purchases labor commands it sometimes with a greater and sometimes with a lesser amount of goods:

"It appears to him dear in the one case, and cheap in the other. In reality, however, it is the goods which are cheap in the one case and dear in the other." [2]

[1] P. 34.   [2] *Ibid.*

The question of an absolute measure or unit of value (whether it is incapable of solution or not) is one which will be avoided in this essay as far as exhaustive or critical discussion is concerned. The purely statical part of the classical theories of value is best considered in isolation, and furthermore the question of an absolute measure is one of such extreme difficulty that it would require a separate essay of much greater dimensions than this history. Malthus examined the question at great length, and Ricardo paid some attention to it. A brief résumé of the classical discussion of this problem will be found in the note at the end of Chapter VII.

It may be of interest to note that Adam Smith virtually contradicts the assertion made in the citation last given by his statement four lines later: " The labourer is rich or poor, is well or ill rewarded, in proportion to the real * * * * price of his labour." [1] This leads to irreconcilable contradictions. Smith has said that a man is rich or poor according to the quantity of labor which his goods enable him to command. That is, the " real value " of a thing is measured by the amount of labor for which it will exchange. Thus a man is rich or poor according to the " real value " of his possessions. A changing physical quantity of goods will have the same " real value " if it command the same quantity of labor. Therefore a given quantity of labor must always exchange for the same amount of *riches* in the sense of this word employed by Smith. If the real wages of a day of labor must always be the same quantity of riches, how can the laborer be richer or poorer according as the physical quantity of the goods of his real wages increases or diminishes? It might be said that Smith means that the laborer will be richer in life's en-

[1] P. 35.

joyments if he receives a larger physical quantity of goods as wages. But Smith is estopped from such a statement because he has affirmed that the measure of *riches* is command of labor or cost in labor, that the more or less of riches can be discovered only by the more or less of the labor commanded by the goods composing the riches.[1]

It is necessary to mention Adam Smith's so-called corn measure of value. Ricardo says, referring to Smith, that " sometimes he speaks of corn, at other times of labour, as a standard measure." [2] The impression thus given is erroneous. Corn is not selected as a standard coördinate with labor, but is merely singled out from among commodities as being a convenient practical index of the real or labor standard. The practical question of corn-rents was interesting and called for some mention. Smith believed that a given quantity of grain possessed more nearly a constant value in different times than most commodities, merely *because* corn is likely to remain from age to age in a steady exchange ratio with *labor*.[3]

---

[1] In criticising the labor-command standard of Smith, Ricardo has made virtually the same point as the above (pp. 8–14, Gonner ed. Ricardo's *Principles*). By *riches* Smith cannot mean what Ricardo means by this term in his famous chapter on the antinomy of value. (Chap. xx, "Value and Riches, their Distinctive Properties.") If by reason of scarcity, wine should come to command in exchange more labor than formerly, Smith would have to say that a given quantity of wine becomes more riches. This Ricardo would not say.

[2] *Principles*, p. 8.

[3] P. 36. The following passage (p. 38) exhibits perfectly Smith's general theory of the relation of labor, the precious metals, and grain to value as a dynamic problem. " Labour, therefore, it appears evidently, is the only universal as well as the only accurate measure of value, or the only standard by which we can compare the values of different commodities at all times and at all places. We cannot estimate, it is allowed, the real value of different commodities from century to century by the quantities of silver which were given for them. We cannot estimate it

from year to year by the quantities of corn. *By the quantities of labour we can, with the greatest accuracy, estimate it both from century to century and from year to year.* From century to century corn is a better measure than silver, *because* from century to century equal quantities of corn will command the same quantity of labour more nearly than equal quantities of silver. From year to year, on the contrary, silver is a better measure than corn, because equal quantities of it will more nearly command the same quantity of labour.''

CHAPTER III

THE EMPIRICAL ACCOUNT OF ADAM SMITH.

1. In the splendid chapters on the " Component Parts of Price," and the " Natural and Market Price of Commodities," Adam Smith flees the more speculative questions of the philosophical essence of value, and turns to that most important, but relatively proximate, principle of exchange value in the modern market, which we now call the law of entrepreneur's costs. It is beyond the scope of this history to follow him through his analysis of the component parts of this cost, called by him the " component parts of price," into wages, profits and rent. The " natural " or " necessary price " is the sum of these components, and is the center toward which actual market-price is always tending. With Cairnes, we now call this by the better term, " normal market value." Nor can we trace the thought into the subsequent separate chapters on " Wages," " Profits," and " Rent of Land," where Adam Smith presents what is probably the earliest attempt at a systematic theory of distribution.

We are concerned only with the fact that in the " empirical account " Adam Smith shifts his ground on the question of the relation of labor to value. While dwelling upon the hypothetical primitive conditions under which the essence of value is supposed to be laid bare, he proposed the *labor-cost* and the *labor-command* standards without a word as to their mutual relations. But as he approaches the problem of value under advanced conditions, he both explains his

---

CHAPTER IV

CRITICISM OF THE THEORIES OF ADAM SMITH.

1. In this chapter it is the intention to examine more fully the reasoning by which Adam Smith sought to establish his main contentions concerning the relation of labor to value. As for a proof that, under " philosophical " primitive conditions, goods would exchange in proportion to their costs in labor, none is given. It is considered obvious that this would be true:

" It is natural that what is usually the produce of two days' or two hours' labour, should be worth double of what is usually the produce of one day's or one hour's labour." [1]

In support of the theorem of the *labor-command standard,* however, in contrast with that of labor-cost, he makes a show of argument, which is contained in the following quotation:

" Every man is rich or poor according to the degree in which he can afford to enjoy the necessaries, conveniences, and amusements of human life. But after the division of labour has once thoroughly taken place, it is but a very small part of those with

[1] P. 49. Torrens, in his *Essay on the Production of Wealth,* has worked out with great pains a form of proof of this proposition. It is exhibited in a series of dialogues between primitive producers to show that an exchange of goods at a ratio out of proportion to labor-costs is incompatible with recognized motives of trade. His proof is good enough under the tacit assumptions which he makes, including all the conditions of the perfect type of fictitious primitive society used by classical writers.

view of the relation of these two standards, and abandons the first one, that of labor cost.   In the primitive state of society, the labor cost of a commodity *determines* the amount of labor commanded by it in exchange.   The two amounts of labor must " naturally " be the same.   The " whole produce of labour," then, belongs to the laborer, and no profits or rent exist to destroy the proportionality between labor-cost and value.   But in society as now constituted, it is different.

" The whole produce of labour does not always belong to the labourer.   He must in most cases share it with the owner of the stock which employs him.   Neither is the quantity of labour commonly employed in acquiring or producing any commodity the only circumstance which can regulate the quantity which it ought commonly to purchase, command, or exchange for.   An additional quantity, it is evident, must be due for the profits of stock," (and the rent of land.) [1]

2. In a word, value in exchange is no longer proportionate to labor-cost, because the value of a commodity must now contain elements which remunerate not only the labor, but also the capital and land employed in its production. Nevertheless, the " real value " of such a commodity produced in advanced society is measured by the labor which that commodity will command in exchange.

" The real value of all the different component parts of price, it must be observed, is measured by the quantity of labour, which they can, each of them, purchase or command.   Labour measures the value not only of that part of price which resolves itself into labour, but of that which resolves itself into rent, and of that which resolves itself into profits." [2]

[1] P. 52.   [2] P. 52.

The inaccuracy of expression in thi Without scrutiny of the context one wo get an idea from the astonishing words ures the *value* of that part of *price* whicl *labour.*"   In the first place, for the la *wages* should be substituted.   Labor is distribution nor a " component part of p ing of the passage is that the " real value even in advanced society, is measured labor which can be had in exchange for fact that its value in exchange is no longe its *cost* of production in labor.   In the abc Smith means to assert that the " real va crete income as a share in distribution is amount of labor it will command.   Thus of the rent of a plot of ground would va according to the number of days of labor tl chased by it in the different years.   As a tl apply to actual life, Adam Smith left us a the law of entrepreneur's cost and a labor- *ure of value.*   But he disowns what is natu as the genuine classical labor theory of value regulates market-value.   This theory was really his alone.[1]

[1] McCulloch and James Mill were but satellites

which a man's own labour can supply him. The far greater part of them he must derive from the labour of other people, and he must be rich or poor according to the quantity of that labour which he can command, or which he can afford to purchase. The value of any commodity, therefore, to the person who possesses it, and who means not to use or consume it himself, but to exchange it for other commodities, is equal to the quantity of labour which it enables him *to purchase or command*. Labour, therefore, is the real measure of the exchangeable value of all commodities." [1]

This passage permits of but one interpretation. If I am rich, in the sense of owning things with a money price or exchange value, in proportion to the quantity of labor which, by means of these things, I can purchase or command, *quantity of labor* here can mean but one thing, namely, quantity of *productive power* as opposed to quantity of toil, pain, subjective sacrifice, or disutility. In society, I am supplied with this world's goods virtually in proportion to the amount of productive power of labor at my call; and this amount is asserted to be the true measure of value. This we may describe as a view of *labor as potential commodity*. Labor to be performed is commodity in the making. What kind of commodity it shall be in the particular case depends upon the will of him who has command over the labor. A later sentence bears out this explanation perfectly:

"[A person's] fortune is greater or less precisely in proportion to the extent of this power [over labor] ; or to the quantity either of other men's labour, or, what is the same thing, of the produce of other men's labour, which it enables him to purchase or command. The exchangeable value of everything must always be precisely equal to the extent of this power which it conveys to its owner." [2]

[1] P. 30.   [2] P. 32.

This signifies, then, that the value of any article to its possessor must be measured by the amount of labor which it can command in exchange, *because* this labor is the means of obtaining valuable articles in general. To Smith, labor is the great homogeneous, undifferentiated, common denominator to the wonderfully diverse mass of goods which come into existence out of it, and the value or " real worth " [1] of each of these goods follows the quantity of the source-stuff turned to its production.

2. The law of supply and demand and the law of entrepreneur's cost are proximate empirical principles which, although possibly of much more practical importance than a philosophy of value, do not give an ultimate explanation of the riddle of this phenomenon. Adam Smith's theory of labor as " potential commodity " is an attempt to give an ultimate explanation, but as such it should be judged a failure, for it really avoids the question of ultimate explanation. It begins: " Every man is rich or poor according to the degree in which he can afford to enjoy the necessaries, conveniences, and amusements of human life." Air is a necessity to human life, but a man is not rich in proportion to the quantity of air he can command. The object of this statement is not to make a carping criticism of Smith, but only to point out that by " necessaries, conveniences and amusements " he means here solely such of these things as have economic value. Since he has already passed judgment that the *economic quantity* of these things is completely independent of the *quantity* of their utility, he sees no way of measuring these things, as economic quantities, except by looking to their origin in a measurable and, as he

[1] When Smith speaks of " exchangeable value " as being measured by power to command labor, he is using the only term he has to stand for any or every concept of value distinct from the " value in use " or general utility of free goods.

believes, homogeneous something called labor.   In criticism
of this we have but to note that if the only means, or the
first means, of determining the *economic quantity* of a
physical complex of goods were by measurement of the labor
turned to its making, the economic system of things would
be turned upside down.   If the value of the articles produced for me by that part of the labor of society over which
I have command, can be determined solely by reference to
the quantity of this labor, I am left without the slightest
guidance for the application of this labor under my direction.   The truth is, the command or direction of labor
necessarily implies the ability to estimate *values* independently of the quantity of labor employed in the production of
them, previously to its employment.   Value is the guiding-
star to labor.   How can the point of attack of labor against
the physical environment be selected unless the results to be
expected in different cases can be compared in value, independently of the quantity of the labor?   If the quantity of
labor determined the value, it would make no difference
where the labor was turned; the value of the result would
always be the same.   Turned in an indefinite number of
directions, labor will produce no value whatsoever; turned
in certain directions it will bring forth the maximum value
of which it is capable.   It is one of the main functions of
the entrepreneur in modern economic society to turn labor-
power in the directions of maximum value return.   All
these things are perfectly obvious, yet value theorists un-
counted have ignored them.   Quantity of labor-cost, even
when conceived of as being an entity of superior homo-
geneity to quantity of satisfaction, cannot be the first or
fundamental means of measuring value.

The view that cost is the essence of value is thus obviously irrational, and no escape from this difficulty is
afforded by the concession made explicitly by Ricardo, and

after him by Marx, that utility is a *condition* prerequisite to value. The problem of directing labor in production is a question of *how much* labor can be economically employed in making such and such a useful thing. In the theories of Ricardo and Marx, the *quantity* of value is held to have no relation to the *quantity* of utility, but to be determined by the quantity of cost. There must be a quantity of utility to which the quantity of productive power destroyed in its obtainment is adjusted. Utility properly conceived, there is such a quantity, and value is its measure.

3. In the first general argument for the labor-command standard, Adam Smith seems to regard labor solely in the aspect of productive power; but, as the reader will recall, we do not advance far in his many-sided discussion before we encounter labor as *disutility*. Labor is later said to be an " invariable measure," because it stands for a constant amount of hardship. Beyond a doubt, *disutility* is associated with value (as "*Bedeutung*") in some very intimate relation.[1] This is, at bottom, the explanation of the remarkable vitality of the labor theory, even in forms that are absurdly incorrect.

If it is my labor which is commanded in exchange by a given commodity, the personal value to me of this commodity for which I have given my labor might well be carried in my mind in terms of the disutility it cost me. So, in a general way, if the amount of some kind of commodity which can be bought by a day's wages (*i. e.,* which " commands " a day's labor) alters, the significance of this commodity to wage-earners in general will alter. Some persons might conceive the change in significance chiefly in

---

[1] Its relation to pure objective exchange-value is another question. In Chapter xi of this essay will be found a summary discussion of the relation of disutility cost to value.

terms of altered disutility cost. This fact is probably considered by statisticians when they investigate questions of real wages, or changes in family budgets. But Adam Smith's proposition that labor commanded in exchange is a precise and invariable measure of *"exchangeable* value" is not a good form of stating so mild a principle.

Further discussion of this subject must be attended by extreme difficulties. For in endeavoring to ascertain what Smith meant, or "ought to have meant," we encounter the difficulties due to the laxness and paucity of Smith's explanations superposed on the difficulties inherent in this intricate subject. His various expressions suggest that his labor theory of value means more than the thought that the disutility of each person's labor may measure the "subjective" value *to that person* of commodities obtained by him in exchange for his own labor.[1] Smith speaks of labor as the "real measure of exchangeable value." The exchange-value of a commodity in a given market is the same, whoever its owner may be and whatever may be his needs, or the relation of this commodity to his particular needs. This relation may give it value *to* him; but we would never speak of the commodity's exchange-value *to* him. This independence of market-value from the particular needs of the particular owner is one of the things desired to be conveyed by the Austrian economists in their term, *"objective* exchange-value." Now Smith fails to distinguish between the "real worth" of goods and their "exchangeable value." There can be no doubt that he would be quite willing to speak of the "real exchangeable value" of a good as being that which is measured by labor.[2] Thus, I be-

[1] The thought in the "final disutility" theories of Gossen, Jevons and Clark, independently worked out by these writers.

[2] These very words were later used by Malthus in his defense of the labor-command standard.

lieve, Smith conceives of a " real worth " independent
of worth to any particular person. This " real worth "
in a good is measurable by the labor commanded in exchange for the good, because, as he first suggests, labor,
as productive power, is the homogeneous source-stuff of
commodities. But secondly, the suggestion enters that
a unit of labor is also a unit of disutility, a unit assumed
to have an independent and invariable significance. This
kind of real worth and such a unit of disutility are
compounded abstractions. No one can hold it against a
concept, except in the infancy of thought, that it is an ab-
straction, but, after my best effort, I for one cannot see that
these concepts are meaningful abstractions.

If we grant this conception of " real worth," and the
conception of a unit of disutility in general, distinguishable
in the different labors of different persons, we still find difficulties ahead. The same commodity may exchange for two
days of common labor or one day of skilled labor. Either
of these is the quantity of labor commanded in exchange.
According to Smith's conception, either must measure its
" real value." Now the fact is, one day of skilled labor
ordinarily involves *less disutility* than two days of common
labor.[1] Competitive wages are paid in proportion to *efficiency,* not in proportion to disutility. A given piece of
labor will count as a great or small quantity when commanded in exchange in proportion to the wages paid for it.
It is then a difficulty with Smith's labor-command standard

---

[1] In this sentence we do not assume the commensurability of disutilities
incurred by different persons, but the commensurability of the disutilities
incident to different occupations. Thus we should all be willing to say
that the steamship stoker's position means harder labor than that of the
chief steward of the dining room, but we may be supposed to judge this
by comparing our own (imagined) labor as a stoker with our own labor
as steward.

that he implies that labor derives its capacity to serve as a measure of real value from its disutility, while the same commodity will command *different* disutilities in different exchanges.   The attempt to reduce skill to disutility by urging that the higher wages of skill are in proportion to the disutility of acquiring the skill is futile.   The tendency of the wages of skilled labor to proportion themselves to the comparative disutility of that labor—*i. e.,* to the sum of the disutility daily felt plus some share or other of the past disutility cost of acquiring the skill—is so completely submerged beneath other forces that it is negligible.   In addition to this, much skill is not acquired, but is inborn without having entailed any disutility cost of acquisition to its possessor.

To conclude with this question, so far as Adam Smith means to suggest that the economic worth of a good to a given person can be measured *by him* in terms of its disutility cost *to him,* the position and some of its consequences mentioned above are well taken.   Smith's theory, however, failed to penetrate the problem as do later theories of the final equivalence of utility and disutility.   But the implications of his arguments further than this seem incapable of defense.

4. Adam Smith states that since under the division of labor any man must derive almost all his necessaries, conveniences and luxuries from the labor of other people, he must be rich, in the sense of possessing things of value, in proportion to the quantity of this labor which he can command.   The assumption implicit in this is that the quantity of labor expended upon the production of things for this man, *as labor-cost,* determines their values.   For if the economic goods obtained by him from the labor of others, which he is enabled to command, should have values out of proportion to the quantity of labor so commanded, namely,

their labor-cost, this man would not be rich or poor merely in proportion to the labor which he commands.   Since, therefore, the labor-command standard of value is made to depend upon labor-cost regulation of value, according to the principal argument advanced by Smith, it follows that Smith is really estopped from applying the labor-command standard as he does under the conditions of advanced society. For he himself has stated that labor-cost regulation of value fails under these conditions.

Adam Smith's *empirical* account of value by no means made future improvement of statement impossible, but it was an excellent theory of proximate principles.   His *philosophical* account was an unsystematic body of suggestions, so filled with difficulties that it is doubtful if the present writer has been able to keep his interpretation and criticism of this account free from fallacy.   The carrying over of the labor-command standard of value from the philosophical to the empirical account seems only to introduce an impurity into the latter.

CHAPTER V

RICARDO AND THE TRUE CLASSICAL LABOR THEORY

1. It is not incumbent upon the historian of a single doctrine to pass judgment upon the question of the proper position of Ricardo as a general economist, compared with Smith and Malthus. But since, in the following chapter, we shall be led to find much fault with Ricardo's method of exposition of the theory of value, it is necessary to state at the outset that Ricardo's writings on value possess the distinctive merit, in contrast with those of Smith and Malthus, that they can be reduced to a whole, essentially self-consistent in its large lines. Self-consistency is not the sole test of truth, and this praise does not signify that Ricardo's is a correct theory, but the longer one studies Ricardo the more satisfactory does his text become, up to the point where one believes he has obtained a complete understanding of it. On the other hand, it is a task of supreme difficulty to read Ricardo critically. His inconsistencies in the use of terms are most trying. It is remarkable that the final result of his reasoning was on the whole self-consistent. The commentator is inclined to quote Senior with approval when he remarked that Mr. Ricardo " is perhaps the most incorrect writer [*i. e.,* in the use of terms] who ever attained philosophical eminence." [1] The point of greatest weight in the labor theory of value, after the vestibule of the subject has been passed through, is treated with a maladroitness which

[1] *Political Economy*, p. 115.

has made a matter that is not over-difficult in itself very hard to understand. This is the theme of sections IV and V of the chapter on value, and is, indeed, in another guise, the difficulty arising out of the " organic composition of capital," which, under this name, becomes the main point of theoretical interest in the third volume of Marx's *Das Kapital*.

There is abundant evidence that Ricardo himself considered the theory of value to be a very hard problem, and furthermore that he was not completely satisfied with his own treatment of it. As late as 1823, he wrote to Mc-Culloch :

" The difficult subject of value has engaged my thoughts, but without my being able satisfactorily to find my way out of the labyrinth." [1]

Earlier he wrote to the same disciple :

" I am not satisfied with the explanation I have given of the principles which regulate value." [2]

Some things have a value which is obviously not regulated by labor cost. Concerning these, Ricardo wrote :

" I cannot get over the difficulty of the wine which is kept in the cellar for three or four years [*i. e.*, while constantly increasing in exchange value], or that of the oak tree, which perhaps originally had not 2 s. expended on it in the way of labour, and yet comes to be worth £100." [3]

2. The writer of the present essay has already acknowl-

---

[1] *Letters of Ricardo to McCulloch*, p. 153.

[2] *Ibid.*, p. 132.

[3] *Letters to McCulloch*, p. 153. This shows that Ricardo was not satisfied in principle with his treatment of the value of scarcity goods.

edged his indebtedness to Professor von Wieser for suggestion of the means of interpreting the main lines of the
history of the labor theory. Professor von Wieser's terse
judgment of Ricardo's writings on value is contained in the
following sentences:

" What, then, did Ricardo attempt? His whole endeavor ex-
hausted itself in trying to show that the philosophical and the
empirical theories of Adam Smith—both of which, indeed, in
taking up this position he had to clear and carry further—did
not contradict each other so much as at first sight would
appear." [1]

The manner of putting this is objectionable, in that it implies, I believe, an improper subordination of Ricardo's
theory to that of Smith. While Ricardo quotes Smith
freely, his exposition of the subject of value is in no sense
a summary and criticism of Smith's views. On the contrary, he writes with a remarkably independent spirit. It
is, nevertheless, true that the principal part of the reasoning
of Ricardo is concerned with the adaptation of the empirical account of value to the philosophical, that is, to the
philosophical account as he understands it. These two accounts are almost inextricably entangled in Ricardo's work,
but their disentanglement is the sole method of exhibiting
the ultimate purport of his reasonings. For, in essence, his
theory is as follows: The value of those things whose value
is subject to an ascertainable principle depends on their cost
of production in human labor. (The value of pure scarcity
goods which cannot be increased in quantity by the application of common human labor simply " varies with the varying wealth and inclinations of those who are desirous to
possess them." [2] If subject to no law of value, these goods

[1] *Natural Value*, Author's Preface, p. xxviii.

[2] *Principles*, Gonner ed., p. 6.

are also, in Ricardo's view, unimportant.)   Labor cost is
the kernel of value, so far as it seems to have a kernel.
This is the philosophical account.   Smith's labor-command
measure is condemned at the outset.   There is little doubt
that labor is here conceived as disutility, though Ricardo
does not pause to discuss the concept of labor.   But
Ricardo's theory ends as an empirical doctrine, in which
labor-cost figures as the regulator of exchange value only
because it is conceived to be the all-important element which
governs the amount of entrepreneur's expenses of production.   Smith abandoned the labor-cost regulator for real
society because he observed that the " necessary price " of
a market commodity, or the price determined by its entrepreneur's cost of production, must cover payments for rent
of land and interest on capital as well as wages of labor.
Not so Ricardo.   He holds fast to the labor-cost standard,
upon the belief that rent does not " enter into " this necessary price, and that the taking of interest causes only a
negligible variation of money cost from proportionality with
labor cost.   The discussion of this variation is the most
involved part of his writings.   The end is an imperfect
reconciliation between the empirical and philosophical accounts.

3. The simpler and more familiar parts of Ricardo's
theory may be considered first.   His doctrine, it should be
observed, is by no means absolute or unconditional.

(1) Utility is a condition essential to value, but no more.
The quantitative discrepancy between utility and exchange
value seems as obvious to Ricardo as to Smith.   In a letter
to Say he expressed his whole theory with respect to utility
even a little more concisely than in the *Principles:*

" The utility of things is incontestibly the *foundation* of their
value, but the degree of their utility cannot be the measure

of their value." " The difficulty of [a thing's] production is
the sole measure of its value." [1]

When arguing against Smith's corn-measure in Chapter
XXVIII (Gonner ed.), our author exclaims: " What can
value have to do with the power of feeding and clothing?"
as if the instantaneous answer should be, " Nothing whatever." This curious slip is mentioned only to show how
far utility was removed from value in Ricardo's habitual
thought.

(2) " Possessing utility, commodities derive their exchangeable value from two sources: from their scarcity,
and from the quantity of labour required to obtain them." [2]
This proposition has occasioned the claim of the " Austrian " writers that the Ricardian theory of value is " dualistic." Not all economists have acquiesced in this criticism,
for there are those who hold the labor-cost and utility theories to be but two parts of one larger, consistent, whole.
Among these latter economists, one of the most uncompromising in his attitude is Professor Heinrich Dietzel, of
Bonn, who asserts that Ricardo's explanation is not dualistic, because the utility and cost views are perfectly reconcilable. [3] Still it appears fair to say that, whether or not some
later writer can construct a theory which is itself not dualistic and which is still in inner harmony with what Ricardo
meant to say, what Ricardo said was dualistic. Textually,
formally, his proposition is dualistic, for an intelligent contemporary reader would interpret his thought as such.
Commodities derive value from two sources, and the law of
the one kind has no applicability to the other kind of goods.

[1] J. B. Say, *Mélanges et Correspondance d'Économie Politique*, Paris,
1833, pp. 93-4.

[2] *Principles*, p. 6.

[3] Dietzel, *Theoretische Socialökonomik*, Leipzig, 1895, pp. 228-30.

(3) The value of scarcity goods is "wholly independent of the quantity of labor originally necessary to produce them." This is because "no labor can increase the supply of such goods." These commodities are, however, an unimportant element in the market.

(4) The labor-cost regulation of values applies only to goods in the production of which competition acts without restraint.

4. The doctrine that, with the foregoing conditions understood, the exchange value of commodities is governed by the comparative quantity of labor required for their production, involves a number of questions with respect to the manner of determining *quantity of labor.* Ricardo did not carry his inquiry into these questions as far as modern critics of the labor theory have pressed theirs, but in the course of his writings he made three important observations on this subject.

(1) In the first place, Ricardo distinguishes between *quantity* and *value* of labor. J. B. Say had in various places endeavored to state Ricardo's position as being that the *value* of labor determines the value of its products, for in this form the doctrine can easily be shown to involve a circle. Ricardo wrote to Say:

"You misrepresent me * * when you say I consider the value of labour to determine the value of commodities; I hold, on the contrary, that it is not the value, but 'the comparative quantity of labour necessary to production which regulates the relative value of the commodities produced.'"[1]

The purport of this—though not so explained by Ricardo—is that the quantity of labor which an entrepreneur is compelled by the nature of a good to employ to produce that

[1] Quoted in *Letters of Ricardo to Malthus*, p. 165, n.

good, determines the amount of wages he has to pay for its production. As far as this single point goes, the answer to Say is satisfactory.

(2) When Marx came to the question of skilled labor, he called it simply " condensed labor." It goes without saying that he judged the degree of the condensation of any concrete skilled labor purely by its comparative wages, or exchange *value*.[1]   Ricardo's treatment of skilled labor is even less satisfactory than Marx's.   He says:

" If a day's labour of a working jeweller be more valuable than a day's labour of a common labourer, it has long ago been adjusted, and placed in its proper position in the scale of value." [2]

What has long ago been adjusted?   In definite words our author does not say, but his meaning is ascertainable.

" If a piece of cloth be now of the value of two pieces of linen, and if, in ten years hence, the ordinary value of a piece of cloth should be four pieces of linen, we may safely conclude, that either more labour is required to make the cloth, or less to make the linen, or that both causes have operated." [3]

If the exchange ratio of cloth to linen alters, the doctrine is that the cause must be that some change has taken place in the quantity of labor required to produce cloth or linen, and *not* that the " value " of a linen-maker's day of labor has changed in ratio to the " value " of a cloth-maker's day.   In other words, if ten

---

[1] For this he is accused of reasoning in a circle. As far as any defense by Marx himself is concerned the charge goes home. Assuming the productivity theory of wages (which is entirely inconsistent with Marx's theory of wages) it is quite permissible to say that labor which has a higher wage (or value) contains more units of productive power, more efficiency units, than that receiving a lower wage.

[2] P. 13.   [3] P. 14.

hours of a cloth-maker's labor have earned the same wages
(and thus occasioned the same cost to entrepreneurs) as
twelve hours of a linen-maker's labor, " we may safely conclude " that it is not alteration of this ratio that causes alteration of the exchange ratio of cloth to linen.   It is this ratio
between the wage-earning capacity of one kind of labor and
another kind that " has long ago been adjusted."   To make
this point perfectly clear, let us quote again:

" The comparative degree of estimation [an equivocal expression which means comparative wage-earning power] in
which the different kinds of human labour are held * * * *
continues nearly the same from one generation to another, or
at least *   *   the variation is very inconsiderable from year
to year, and therefore can have little effect, for short periods,
on the relative value of commodities." [1]

The question is this: In the labor-cost theory of value,
does skilled labor count as *more* labor per day than unskilled, and if so upon what principle?   Ricardo's argument, as just traced, avoids the question, and is faulty in
two essential points.   In the first place, it is not true, and
was not true in Ricardo's time, that the comparative skilful-
ness of labor employed in producing different commodities
remains unchanged.   Machine invention alone produces
veritable revolutions in this field.   But in the second place
(a more important point as a matter of theory), in this
argument Ricardo has shifted his ground with respect to
the meaning of his labor-cost law.   This principle is stated
in italics at the head of his chapter:

" The value of a commodity, or the quantity of any other
commodity for which it will exchange, depends on the relative
quantity of labour which is necessary for its production."

[1] P. 16.

This means precisely that, if one A exchange for two B, it is because, *at this time, without reference to changes in time,* it costs twice as much labor to produce an A as to produce a B. But now Ricardo has virtually changed the principle to mean that *alterations* in the exchange ratios of commodities will be due to *alterations* in the comparative amounts of labor required to produce them. This is a different principle, and indeed one no stronger than the other. We are forced to the conclusion that Ricardo unconsciously avoided the real question in the case, and failed to explain away the difficulty of skilled labor in the labor theory.

(3) The quantity of labor required in the production of a commodity, which regulates its value, includes the labor employed in making the raw material, machinery and buildings (capital goods) used up in its production, as well as the labor directly applied to it. This proposition is copiously illustrated by examples drawn from primitive and modern industry, and commands immediate assent. It is obvious, when once stated, that the labor indirectly applied to the production of a commodity is no less *required,* if we are to obtain it, than that directly applied.

5. We have here an important consideration. If the labor *directly* applied to the production of a commodity were all that is included in its labor-cost, the entrepreneur's expenses, covering cost to him of machinery and raw material, would be too obviously out of proportion to the labor cost (as manifested in *his* wages cost). But it is Ricardo's intention to reduce the cost of capital goods to labor cost. The total labor cost of a commodity produced from capital and raw material is paid for by a series of entrepreneurs in their wages charges. Each entrepreneur exacts a " profit " for the time he has advanced the wages. It is in this way, as Ricardo sees it, that interest enters into entrepreneur's costs. Does it destroy the force of labor

cost as a regulator of exchange value? To make Ricardo's answer to this question clear, it is necessary to refer first to what he has to say in Chapter IV of the *Principles* on natural and market price.

The term "Natural Price" has, it happens, a "philosophical" and an "empirical" significance. It is at best an inexact pair of words. Its empirical meaning is simply *normal value,* the excellent term for that value which, under competition, constitutes a center of oscillation for market values. Its "philosophical" meaning, as suggested a few times by Smith, is the *human cost* of obtaining goods from the physical outer world.

> "Labour was the first price, the original purchase-money that was paid for all things. It was not by gold or by silver, but by labour, that all the wealth of the world was originally purchased."

With this sort of natural or primary price Adam Smith's empirical chapter on "Natural and Market Price" has nothing to do. This ought also to be true of Ricardo's chapter (Chapter IV), because it is a chapter explaining how competition always forces the market-price toward a normal value.[1] It turns out in the end that this normal value is a sum of exchange value which is just sufficient to cover the *wages* of labor and the *interest* of capital required in production. This is never made clear. Malthus probably never understood Ricardo as meaning this. What we affirm is, that *his text* means this when it is altered or rectified so as to give it the self-consistency which seems to lie within it.

6. We need now the proof of this interpretation. The

---

[1] This explanation of the workings of competition is beautifully written both by Smith and Ricardo—is *classic* in fact.

opening sentence of the chapter on natural and market price proceeds as follows:

" In making labour the foundation of the value of commodities, and the comparative quantity of labour which is necessary to their production the rule which determines the respective quantities of goods which shall be given in exchange for each other, we must not be supposed to deny the accidental and temporary deviations of the actual or market price of commodities from *this, their primary and natural price.*" [1]

This sentence seems to state that the labor cost of a commodity is its " natural price." If so, the statement is due to the influence of the philosophical account; but it is an absurdity in this connection. Actual market-price does not deviate temporarily from *labor cost.* Normal value is not an amount of labor, nor can it be spoken of as equal to an amount of labor. The passage is a careless way of saying that the normal values of goods are *in proportion to* their labor costs. Ricardo's real conception of normal value is this: The total labor cost of a commodity determines the total wages charges that must be paid by the entrepreneur, or series of entrepreneurs producing it. Competition tends to give the entrepreneurs producing different commodities equal rates of " profits " upon these outlays. Therefore the normal exchange value of a commodity is composed of a sum of wages costs (due to the nature of the commodity as requiring such and such an amount of labor to produce it), which is the independent determining element, and a sum of interest which is merely a uniform rate upon the wages cost. It is in this way that labor cost regulates value, *according to an empirical account.* [2]

[1] P. 65. The italics are the present writer's.
[2] " It is necessary for me to remark that I have not said because one

To substantiate this view of Ricardo's meaning, we can quote the following:

" Mr. Malthus appears to think that it is a part of my doctrine that the cost and value of a thing should be the same;—it is, if he means by cost, ' cost of production ' including profits." [1]

The only kind of cost that includes " profits " (*i. e.*, interest) is entrepreneur's cost.

7. We may now turn our attention to what is perhaps as difficult a passage as was ever incorporated into a treatise on economics. I refer to Sections IV and V of Chapter I of Ricardo's *Principles*. These sections treat of the *complication of interest* in the labor theory of value. [2] But if all Ricardo claims in his labor theory is that normal values are *in proportion to* labor costs, why is not the explanation satisfactory that interest is merely a rate taken upon wages costs? The difficulty is that in reality two commodities may cost the same amount of wages (because, as Ricardo has it, they require the same amount of labor for production) and yet cost very different amounts of interest. In such a case the two commodities have the same labor costs but have different entrepreneur's costs, and consequently

commodity has so much labour bestowed upon it as will cost £1,000 and another so much as will cost £2,000 that therefore one would be of the value of £1,000 and the other of the value of £2,000, but I have said that their value will be to each other as two to one, and that in those proportions they will be exchanged. It is of no importance to the truth of this doctrine whether one of these commodities sells for £1,100 and the other for £2,200, or one for £1,500 and the other for £3,000," *etc.* Gonner ed., p. 39.

[1] *Principles*, p. 39, n.   The same statement is made in *Letters to Trower*, p. 153.

[2] The difficulty of rent is escaped through the Ricardian theory of rent. The present writer is persuaded that the classical theory of rent is unsound in this respect.

different exchange values. This comes about because the entrepreneur (or series of entrepreneurs) who produces commodity A may have been compelled to pay the money wages to the labor producing it a longer time before A can be put on the market than is the case with commodity B, though the *amount* of wages paid in both cases be the same.

8. In the end, Ricardo's theory of the interest difficulty reduces itself to the statement that has just been finished. That is to say, the above is the true interpretation of his argument. But Ricardo's own presentation of the difficulty is superficially so different from this statement that it will be necessary to prove this interpretation in detail. (1) In the first place, he separates the general case of " profits " paid on a longer " advance " of wages into three subdivisions.

"According as capital is rapidly perishable, and requires to be frequently reproduced, or is of slow consumption, it is classed under the heads of circulating or of fixed capital." ("A division not essential, and in which the line of demarcation cannot be accurately drawn."—Note.)

" Two trades may employ the same amount of capital; but it may be very differently divided with respect to the portion which is fixed, and that which is circulating." "A rise in the wages of labour cannot fail to affect unequally commodities produced under such different circumstances" (in respect to the proportions of these two kinds of capital in different trades.) [1]

Section V is written to show that different degrees of durability in the durable capital have the same effect as different proportions of the durable to the circulating capital, and is merely an example of the bad arrangement of

[1] Pp. 24–6.

the *Principles*.[1] Formally, there is a third case. Goods
slower to market must bring more "profit." But all cases
come to the same thing, *i. e.,* a longer investment of entrepreneur's "capital" in labor, before the commodity produced can be put finally upon the market.

(2) In the second place, the effect of all this, says
Ricardo, is to introduce a *second cause of variation of*
"relative values." The

"variety in the proportions in which the two sorts of capital
may be combined introduces another cause, besides the greater
or less quantity of labour necessary to produce commodities, for
the variations in their relative value—this cause is the rise or
fall in the value of labour."[2]

A rise in wages affects "relative values," because wages,
being a different fractional part of the entrepreneur's costs
of different commodities, the *whole* of entrepreneur's costs
is affected in varying degrees by the increase of this one
factor. In Ricardo's view a rise of wages means simply a
fall of profits. If the entrepreneur's cost of production of
good A were ½ wages and ½ "profits," and of good B ¾
wages and ¼ "profits," then if general wages rise a fixed
percentage, and consequently general "profits" fall a fixed
percentage, it follows that the entrepreneur's costs of A
and B will change, one relatively to the other, though the
costs of these goods in labor are not altered. He concludes:

"It appears that in proportion to the durability of capital employed in any kind of production, the relative prices of these
commodities on which such durable capital is employed, will
* * fall as wages rise, and rise as wages fall; and on the

---

[1] The distinction between the two kinds of capital was stated to be a
question of degree in the first section on this subject.

[2] P. 24.

contrary those which are produced chiefly by labour with less fixed capital, or with fixed capital of a less durable character than the medium in which price is estimated, will rise as wages rise, and fall as wages fall." [1]

9. Ricardo's way of describing the interest difficulty is unnecessarily roundabout, but a more important point is that it is positively misleading. He must mean that interest and wages together make up entrepreneur's costs. In the cost of producing one commodity interest will be a certain fraction of the whole; in the cost of producing another commodity it will be a different fraction. Now, says Ricardo, if the general rate of interest or of wages rises or falls, it will affect the total cost of production of two such commodities in different degrees. [2] Thus a rise or fall of the general rate of wages of labor is a cause of variation of the exchange ratios of products, as well as the cause of changes in the quantity of labor required to produce them. This statement is misleading, because the existence of interest throws the entrepreneur's costs, and consequently the normal values of commodities, out of proportion to their labor costs without any reference to *variations* in the general rates of interest or of wages. *At any given time* values are already out of proportion to labor costs, whether or not there be a future change of the ratio of wages; yet Ricardo is misled in his illustrations to assume the proportionality before the wages rate changes. [3] The origin of Ricardo's

[1] P. 35.

[2] Ricardo's theory that a rise of interest must accompany a fall of wages and *vice versâ* is not an essential part of the present problem. Interest acts as a cause of deviation of exchange value from proportionality to wages cost, whether this particular theory of wages and interest be adopted or not.

[3] Compare the same unconscious shifting of ground in the discussion of skilled labor.

indirection in explaining the law of entrepreneur's costs lies in the preconceptions of the "philosophical" account of value. To be precise, it is due to Ricardo's quarrel with one of Smith's two "philosophical" standards, namely, the labor-command standard. According to this standard, if wages rise or fall, the amount of a given commodity required to command a day of labor in exchange falls or rises. Smith said, in effect, that the "exchangeable value" of commodities in general falls when wages rise. He could not have meant pure exchange value by this, but Ricardo took him at his word, and proceeded to show that when the exchange ratio between day labor and a commodity alters, the exchange value of the labor may change just as much as that of the commodity. Therefore he concluded early in his chapter that the exchange value of commodities depends on the comparative quantity of labor required for their production, and not (as Adam Smith said) on the greater or less compensation which is paid for that labor.[1] On account of this dispute, he is led to state the qualification of the labor-cost law, due to interest, in terms of variation of the compensation of labor. That is, he qualifies slightly his original statement against Smith. The false philosophy that labor cost is the *essence* of value exercised an influence upon the statement of the empirical law of costs which was truly baleful in English political economy. Its effect on terminology reached at least into the writings of John Stuart Mill, who sometimes referred to cost of production as being composed of *labor and profits!* [2] Either wages and profits (interest), or labor and abstinence, but not labor and profits!

10. What Ricardo should have given us is a rectilinear

[1] P. 5. *Principles.*

[2] See also Ricardo, himself: "The value of almost all commodities is made up of labor and profits." *Letters to Malthus*, p. 225.

theory of entrepreneur's costs. For a theory of these costs
is truly all he has offered. As for an ultimate answer to
the riddle of value—an answer not contained in the simple
empirical law of costs—Ricardo has not given us one. For,
in answer to the query, *why* labor cost, barring the qualifications he develops, should regulate value, he has said nothing. He has not even said what labor is; and in explaining
the ultimate nature of economic value, and the relation of
labor to it, it will not suffice to trust that every one knows
exactly what is meant by labor. It should be understood,
without remark, that the criticisms here passed are not in
the least directed against his greatness as a thinker. His
greatness is relative to his time. We criticize him with
reference to the developed theory of our time; if we did not
do this, this history would be a mere summary of Ricardo's
chapter on value, and would be almost, if not quite, pointless.

To conclude, Ricardo makes four qualifications of the
doctrine of the labor-cost regulation of value. (1) Labor
must be expended on things of utility. Utility is an absolute condition of value. (2) Goods to be subject to this
law of value must be reproducible. The unimportant class
of scarcity goods has a value entirely independent of labor-
cost. (3) Labor-cost really regulates only the natural or
central value of goods. There must be perfect competition
to keep the market value at the natural value. (4) Variety
in the proportions of fixed and circulating employer's capital causes an aberration of natural value from proportion
to pure labor-cost.

These points reappear explicitly or implicitly in all labor
accounts of value. They are interesting in view of the
estimates of Ricardo's theory as being absolute. The second
and fourth counts especially negative this estimate. The
point of greatest interest in this connection is the question

as to how much of a trunk remains of the Ricardian labor theory after so much bark has been stripped off. Ricardo considered the theory to remain for practical purposes intact. The fourth count is the only one that gives him serious concern, and though he is plainly much impressed with the force of the difficulty while he is treating of it, and concludes because of it that labor is not a precise regulator of value, when he has delivered himself of this statement he proceeds with the resolve to abstract from the whole difficulty, and reason as if the thesis first advanced were unqualified.

" In estimating, then, the causes of the variations in the value of commodities, although it would be wrong wholly to omit the consideration of the effect produced by a rise or fall of labour [1] it would be equally incorrect to attach much importance to it; and consequently, in the subsequent part of this work, though I shall occasionally refer to this cause of variation, I shall consider all the great variations which take place in the relative value of commodities to be produced by the greater or less quantity of labour which may be required from time to time to produce them." [2]

This citation from the *Principles,* edition of 1821, indicates the position Ricardo usually took. But occasionally he appears to have wavered regarding the proper emphasis of the qualification. For instance, in 1820 he wrote: " I sometimes think that if I were to write the chapter on value again which is in my book, I should acknowledge that the relative value of commodities was regulated by two causes instead of by one, namely, by the relative quantity of labour necessary to produce the commodities in question *and by*

[1] *i. e.*, wages.
[2] P. 34.

the rate of profit " . . .[1] Ricardo's theory of value, as qualified by himself, might be summarized: Objects of utility, " produced by labor " (the function of factors in production other than labor not explained), and capable of further production by the application of more labor, have normal values in proportion to the total quantity of labor required to produce them, except that this proportionality is disturbed " by the employment with labor of capital of various degrees of durability."

NOTE. Ricardo's principle of rent is susceptible of development into a universal principle of competitive distribution. To J. B. Clark this development is in fact due. (In divers early articles in the American economic periodicals. Professor Clark's views have now been summed up in his *Distribution of Wealth*. See especially Chapters iv, viii, xii and xiii.) Perfecting the reasoning, by means of which Ricardo endeavored to get rid of the rent of land, as a cause of the divergence of the exchange value of products from proportionality to their labor costs, Clark gets rid of interest on capital as well. What is left of the product of industry after interest (including land rent and rent of other capital goods) has been deducted is defined by Professor Clark as the *specific* product of labor, or the marginal product of labor. To assert proportionality of the specific product of labor to its labor cost is a very different thing from asserting that the total product of land, labor and capital in any given business is governed by the labor cost of that product, defining the labor cost as Ricardo did. It cannot be said that Ricardo in any way realized that the principle of land rent could be turned to account as a universal principle in determining shares in distribution. But there is a distant hint at such use in the following passage: "The exchangeable value of all commodities, whether they be manufactured, or the produce of the mines, or the produce of land, is always regulated, not by the less quantity of labour that will suffice for their production under circumstances highly favourable, and exclusively enjoyed by those who have peculiar facilities of production, but by the greater quantity of labour necessarily bestowed on their production by those who have no such facilities, by those who continue to produce them under the most unfavourable circumstances, meaning by the most unfavourable circumstances, the most unfavourable under which the quantity of produce required, renders it necessary to carry on the production." (P. 50.) In

[1] *Letters to McCulloch*, p. 71.

Chapter xi of the present essay we shall attempt to make clear the difference between the assertion that the exchange value of the entire product of a given industry is determined by its labor cost and an assertion that the specific product of labor has a value determined by its labor cost.

The following chapters will contain many references to Ricardo. These will concern minor points in his theory which are best taken up in connection with the arguments of subsequent economists.

y not be proved by a new det...
, milk, suet, and stones is a plu...
t plums. Upon this principle M...
how that commodities do really
cording to the quantity of labour
must be acknowledged that in the
n he has not been deterred by ap-

lloch's definition of labor, the ex-
upon it involve an uncommonly
ng included in labor any of the
," which tend to produce a desir-
to place aside desirable natural
atuitous." [2]   Having no way to
ons by themselves, he decides, in
ommodity is found which possesses
xcess of that which would be pro-
human labor, the thing to do is to
natural forces to restore the desired
quently he adopted another line of
with this one, but his later method
olute truth of the labor-cost theory
e. [3]
ty in which the Marxian theory of
o the fact, as Marx described it, that
sition of capital" is, for technical
ifferent industries, is the same as the
nd circulating" capital, which occu-
of Ricardo's and McCulloch's atten-
as discussed by Marx differs from

pp. 100-101.
of Nations, vol. iv, pp. 77-78.
o. 371-3.

CHAPTER VI

M'CULLOCH, JAMES MILL AND TORRENS.   ANTICIPATIONS OF MARX'S THIRD VOLUME.

1. THE three minor writers, McCulloch, James Mill, and, to a less degree, Torrens, were imitative expounders of the Ricardian political economy.   While their views were not identical with those of Ricardo, they were accustomed to explain themselves by pointing out wherein they differed from the master.   In this history they are of interest because each endeavored to state the labor-cost theory in a more arbitrary form than did Ricardo himself.   This chapter could well be entitled, " The Labor Theory Running Riot."   McCulloch and Mill endeavored to reason out of existence the qualification Ricardo placed in the doctrine on account of interest, and Torrens thought he avoided the difficulty by stating that value is determined by cost in " accumulated labor."   An interesting fact in the literary history of the labor theory, and one which, to the best of my knowledge, has not hitherto been brought to light, is that McCulloch anticipated Karl Marx's solution of the " organic composition of capital " problem.   Marx closed his theory of value, in the first volume of *Das Kapital*, with the confession that, to all *appearances,* the facts of market values contradict the theory.   He promised, however, to show, in a later volume, that in *reality* there is no contradiction.[1]   When the second volume appeared only to defer

[1] *Das Kapital*, 1st ed., pp, 285, 286, 508, n. See Böhm-Bawerk, *Karl Marx and the Close of his System*, p. 24.

to the third the promised solution, "a regular prize essay contest" sprang up in Germany, and endured for ten years, in which the participants endeavored to forecast what Marx's solution would be. No one was successful.[1] The answer to the enigma, as it appeared in the posthumous third volume of *Das Kapital,* is precisely the one McCulloch gave to the same question.

I. McCULLOCH.

2. We shall not retrace the general lines of Ricardo's exposition as they reappear in McCulloch's writings.[2] In the course of the numerous editions of his *Principles,* and in his other observations upon value, this writer managed to commit nearly every conceivable blunder that could connect itself with the labor theory.[3] From time to time, Ricardo mildly reproved his disciple for his rigidity:

"You go a little farther than I go in estimating the value of commodities by the quantity of labour required to produce them. You appear to admit of no exception or qualification whatever, whereas I am always willing to allow that some of the variations in the relative value of commodities may be referred to causes distinct from the quantity of labour necessary to produce them."[4]

[1] Böhm-Bawerk, *op. cit.,* p. 26.

[2] The writings herein referred to are his *Principles of Political Economy,* 4th ed., Edinb., 1849, and his extensive notes on Adam Smith's text in the McCulloch edition of the *Wealth of Nations,* 4 vols., Edinb., 1828.

[3] In his *Capital and Interest,* pp. 97–102, Böhm-Bawerk devotes a few pages to McCulloch's theory of interest, which is interwoven with his theory of value. Böhm-Bawerk concludes: "McCulloch's utterances on the subject are one great collection of incompleteness, irrationality and inconsistency." The examples of McCulloch's reasonings cited by Böhm-Bawerk show the above judgment to be scrupulously just.

[4] *Letters of Ricardo to McCulloch (Pub. Am. Econ. Assn.,* Vol. 10), pp. 131–2.

"There is nothing that ma tion. A composition of flour pudding; if by stones be mea McCulloch undertakes to exchange for each other a employed upon them: and i instance which he has chos parent difficulties."[1]

Should we grant McCu planations which he base "vicious" circle. Havi operations of all "natur able result, he is force operations that are "g measure natural operati effect, that whenever a an exchange value in e portionate to its cost in add in enough labor of proportionality. Subse reasoning, incompatible of establishing the abs was of the same calibr

3. The fatal difficu value culminated, due the "organic compos reasons, different in difficulty of "fixed pied so large a share tion. The problem

[1] Malthus, *Definitions,*
[2] McCulloch ed. *Wealth*
[3] *Principles,* 4th ed., p

Ricardo's greatly in terminology, and considerably in certain other external features, but the identity of the two in essence can easily be shown.

From his general law that the value of a commodity is governed by its labor cost,[1] Marx made a law of wages follow as a corollary, namely, that the value of labor, its exchange-value, or wages, is governed by its cost of production in labor. It is very hard to find a labor-cost of production of labor, so, by an act of logical legerdemain, this becomes the labor-cost of labor's *subsistence.*[2]   The value *produced by* labor depends upon the duration of its exertion; but, says Marx, the *exchange value of* labor is a different thing. If laborers commonly work ten hours a day for their employers, while six hours of labor will produce a day's *subsistence,* the value produced by a day of labor is as ten, while the wages paid for it are—in virtue of the general law of value—as six.   The difference between the value produced by labor and the value of labor—in this case (adopting the labor-cost unit of value) four hours of value—is the famous "*surplus-value,*" and the four hours a day is called the surplus labor time.   We shall have to adopt a special and *purely temporary* terminology to describe the complication in this theory about to be discovered.[3]   By value we mean

---

[1] We omit the qualification regarding "socially necessary" labor, and the theory of skilled labor as "condensed labor," as not required for our present point.

[2] If one granted, for the sake of argument, both the labor-cost law of value and the iron law of wages, we should still lack the slightest justification for deriving the latter as a corollary from the former.   The only theoretical basis of the iron law of wages is a rigid Malthusian law of population, or labor supply, the alleged law so greatly abhorred by Marx and all socialists.

[3] The elaborate special terminology developed by Marx for the problem (not followed here) will be found explained in full in Böhm-Bawerk's

exchange-value, unless otherwise specified. The outlay of value made by an entrepreneur in labor, raw-material, machinery, *etc.,* returns to him in the course of time a certain value of products, which is greater than the outlay required to produce them. The excess of this value over the outlay we shall call the " profit fund." Now, according to Marx, *surplus-value is the sole source of this profit fund.* The reasoning to support this runs as follows: The entrepreneur's investments in machinery and raw-material, says Marx, cannot contribute anything to this fund. For, according to the labor dialectic, all the value these goods can contribute to their products is derived from their own labor-costs, and the law of value forces the entrepreneur to pay this value for them in full. They can, therefore, afford him no surplus. But the *labor* he buys is a different kind of thing. It, and it only, as just explained, gives more value to the product than he is forced by the law of value to pay for it.

We are now face to face with the great difficulty. If surplus-value is the sole source of the profit fund, the profit funds of different business units ought to be in proportion to the surplus labor time immediately exploited in them. Since the surplus labor time in each day of labor depends on the general rate of wages, there is a general rate of surplus labor time per labor day—*e. g.,* four hours in ten—and the profit fund of every business would be directly in proportion to the number of laborers it employed. This is absolutely not the case in fact. " It appears, therefore," says Marx,

excellent essay previously cited. This little book presents Marx's theory of value, the "contradiction" and the outcome, in the clearest possible form. It would be useless to infringe on the territory covered by this work, but Dr. v. Böhm-Bawerk did not mention the existence of the same "contradiction" in classical English theory.

"that here the theory of value is irreconcilable with the actual movement of things." [1]

For technical reasons, the proportions in which the entrepreneur's outlays are invested in labor on the one hand, and other production-goods on the other hand, are different in different lines of business. The make-up of the entrepreneur's outlay with respect to these proportions Marx calls the " organic composition " of his capital. [2] The facts of life are that equal capitals, in the sense of equal outlays, in different employments tend to produce equal " profit funds," regardless of their organic composition. Now what the profit fund actually turns out to be, depends on the selling price or value of the product. If we take a capital spent *in large proportion* for labor, the large amount of surplus labor time exploited ought to give the product a value very much in excess of the outlay, and afford a large profit fund. If we take a precisely equal capital, spent in very small proportion for labor, and almost entirely for machinery, *etc.,* the relatively small amount of surplus labor time exploited ought to make the value of the product not nearly so great as that of the first capital.

Since Marx frankly admits that in fact competition makes *the value of these products equal instead of unequal,* how does he " solve the contradiction " and redeem his theory? The actual " profit " (as defined here temporarily) afforded by the selling-value of the products is, throughout society, on the average, say 20 per cent. of that value. Where the " organic composition of capital " in a particular industry happens to be such that the profit which ought to

---

[1] *Das Kapital*, v. iii, p. 131; quoted by Böhm-Bawerk, *op. cit.*, p. 49.

[2] "Die organische Zusammensetzung 'des Kapitals," *Das Kapital*, vol. iii, p. 124.

be produced according to the theory is also the actual profit, here the *value* of the product required by the theory will be the same as the actual value. But in some industries where the proportion of labor purchased in the total outlay is low, the actual value will be above the theoretical value, whereas in other industries, under reverse conditions, the actual value will be below the theoretical value. Now, concludes Marx, *the variations of actual values* (called by Marx simply " prices ") *above and below the theoretical or labor values* (called by Marx simply " values ") *counterbalance or cancel one another, and the total actual values of all commodities collectively remain equal to their total labor values.*[1]

The "theoretical values," so-called above, are those which would be in proportion to labor costs. The law of labor cost declares that the value of any given commodity is determined by its cost in labor. In admitting that in fact actual particular values do not follow this law, Marx has abandoned the law. (For a consideration of the erroneous claim that the average rate of surplus-value determines the average rate of profits, the reader may refer to Böhm-Bawerk's essay.)

The point desired to be made here, is that Ricardo's difficulty of " fixed and circulating " capital is the same as that in the Marxian theory. Ricardo stated that variations in the proportions in which fixed and circulating capitals are combined in different industries introduces a second cause of change in the relative value of a commodity. The first

[1] Vol. iii, p. 138. See Böhm-Bawerk, *op. cit.*, p. 67 *et seq.* There are other arguments advanced by Marx for the redemption of his theory, considered in order by Böhm-Bawerk, but that given is the first and principal one. The second is that the law of value governs the *movement of prices*. This is analogous to, if not identical with, Ricardo's claim, that changes in labor-cost are the causes of changes of values. See *ante*, pp. 54-5.

cause is change in the quantity of labor required to produce a commodity; the second is a change in the general rate of wages. In the chapter in this history devoted to Ricardo, it has been argued at length [1] that what Ricardo said was only a round-about explanation of the fact that the values required by the labor theory are not the same as actual values.

McCulloch, following Ricardo, discusses the same problem in the same way, and concludes that changes in the rate of wages will cause variations of values aside from the influence of pure labor cost. But he adds to what Ricardo has said, attempting a justification of the pure labor-cost theory on the grounds that it regulates average value. I trust what has been said will make it clear that McCulloch's defense is identical in essence with that of Marx, though different in form. McCulloch wrote as follows, in 1849:

" It should also be observed, that though fluctuations in the rate of wages occasion some variation in the exchangeable value of *particular* commodities, they neither add to nor take from the *total value* of the entire mass of commodities. If they increase the value of those produced by the least durable capitals, they equally diminish the value of those produced by the more durable capitals. Their aggregate value continues, therefore, always the same. And though it may not be strictly true of a particular commodity, that its exchange value is directly as its cost, or as the quantity of labour required to produce it and bring it to market, it is most true to affirm this of the *mass of commodities taken together*." [2]

McCulloch also expressed the same thought twenty-one years earlier, in 1828. Though a change of the rate of wages may cause a particular commodity to vary from its " real value,"

[1] Pp. 55 *et seq.*

[2] *Principles*, 4th ed., p. 371 (1849). The italics are mine.

"the exchangeable value of some other commodity must vary to the same extent in a contrary direction." [1]

Marx says the same, and concludes that the variations of the actual from the theoretical values cancel one another.[2] Both McCulloch and Marx were involved in a hopeless endeavor to overcome the difficulty of interest.

2. JAMES MILL.

4. James Mill held that value depends, in the first instance, on demand and supply, but ultimately upon cost of production.[3]   Cost of production consists of cost in capital and labor combined, but the capital element can be reduced to labor, and in the last resort quantity of labor cost determines the exchange value of commodities.[4]   But there is an argument which is brought to controvert this conclusion.

"It is said that the exchangeable value of commodities is affected by time, without the intervention of labour; because, when profits of stock must be included, so much must be added for every portion of time which the production of one commodity requires beyond that of another." [5]

Mill takes the regular example of the cask of wine, worth twenty sacks of flour now—because it cost the same amount of labor—but worth more if kept in a cellar some years.

---

[1] McCulloch edition of the *Wealth of Nations*, vol. iv, note viii, p. 200.

[2] "Dass die Abweichungen vom Werth . . . sich gegeneinander aufheben." *Das Kapital*, vol. iii, p. 140. James Mill, in *Elements of Political Economy*, pp. 112-113 (1826), said the same thing. When the general rate of wages varies, for "the aggregate of commodities, taken all together, there is neither fall nor rise."

[3] *Elements of Political Economy*, London, 1826. This statement probably came from Malthus, who laid down the general lines of the theory of value in this same way in 1820.

[4] P. 96.   [5] Pp. 96-7.

Now, he says, the objection here is that there is an addition of value without an application of more labor, and that therefore quantity of labor does not regulate value. But

"this objection is founded on a misapprehension with respect to the nature of profits. Profits are, in reality, the measure of quantity of labour; and the only measure of quantity of labour to which, in the case of capital, we can resort. This can be established by rigid analysis. If two commodities are produced, a bale of silk, for example, for immediate consumption, and a machine, which is an article of fixed capital; it is certain, that if the bale of silk and the machine were produced by the same quantity of labour, and in the same time, they would exactly exchange for one another: quantity of labour would clearly be the regulator of their value. But suppose that the owner of the machine, instead of selling it, is disposed to use it, for the sake of the profits which it brings; what is the real character and nature of his action? Instead of receiving the price of his machine all at once, he takes a deferred payment, so much per annum: he receives, in fact, an annuity, in lieu of the capital sum; an annuity fixed by the competition of the market, and which *is therefore an exact equivalent for the capital sum.* Whatever the proportion which the capital sum bears to the annuity, whether it be ten years' purchase, or twenty years' purchase, such a proportion is each year's annuity of the original value of the machine. The conclusion therefore is incontrovertible: as the exchangeable value of the machine, had it been sold as soon as made, would have been the practical measure of the quantity of labour employed in making it, one-tenth or one-twentieth of that value measures also a tenth or a twentieth of the quantity of labour."[1]

When an entrepreneur pays a certain sum for a machine, which he uses up in production, at the end a certain sum of value produced stands in the place of, and is imputed to, the

[1] Pp. 99–100. The italics are mine.

destroyed machine.   This sum of value is normally greater
than the value of the machine, being sufficient, in fact, to replace the machine and leave a marginal fund of value, which
we call interest.   But Mr. Mill's text discloses the fact that
it is the gross value of the product of the machine which he
designates by the term " profit."   If the machine lasts ten
years, the entrepreneur receives these gross profits in ten
annual installments.   In purchasing the machine he has remunerated the labor which was expended in its production.
Now he receives back that remuneration in ten parts.   *Competition makes these ten parts the "equivalent" of the original whole.*

" It thus appears that profits are simply remuneration for
labour.   They may, indeed, without doing any violence to
language, hardly even by a metaphor, be denominated wages :
the wages of that labour which is applied, not immediately by
hand, but mediately by the instruments which the hand has
produced." [1]

Such was the puzzle of value in " classical " times that a
thinker of repute could resort to explanations shallow almost
beyond belief.   It is the italicized line, of course, which
begs the question.   The assertion that the gross return from
a machine is the exact *equivalent* of its cost price, might
mean that the sum total of the " annuities," in which the
entrepreneur receives this return, is *equal* to the cost price
of the machine to him.   In this case the statement is simply
false.   But if the intention be to admit that the sum of
annuities is more than equal to the cost price, the plain import of the admission is unconsciously concealed under the
word "*equivalent.*"   For the excess of the value of the
product of the machine which affords this surplus in the

[1] Pp. 102-3.

annuities is precisely the value out of proportion to the cost
of the product in labor indirectly applied to it, that is, applied through the machine.   To return to the cask of wine,
by hypothesis, its value is in excess of proportionality to the
quantity of labor it has cost.   And yet Mr. Mill sets about
to explain that its value is, nevertheless, in proportion to the
quantity of labor it has cost, because it is a general principle
that " profits " are " really wages of labour."   In fact,

" the case of the wine in the cellar coincides exactly with that
of a machine worn out in a year, which works by itself without
additional labour.   The new wine, which is one machine is
replaced by its produce, the old wine, with that addition of
value which corresponds with the return to capital employed
upon the land [in Mill's view, the capital that sets the rate of
interest for all other] ; and the account which is to be rendered
of the one return, is also the true account of the other." [1]

Although Mr. Mill has taken trouble to show that it is a
misapprehension to suppose that difference in the time required to produce commodities throws their values out of
proportion to their labor costs, he now caps the climax of
his strange argument by explaining, directly after Ricardo,
how a rise or fall in the general rate of wages will alter the
exchange ratios of commodities, irrespective of changes in
their labor costs.   As explained in the chapter on Ricardo,
this is but an indirect way of showing that the existence of
interest is fatal to the law of labor cost, and that the length
of time through which interest must be taken is a material
factor in determining the cost of production of commodities.   The failure of Mr. Mill, as a disciple of Ricardo, to
understand the real meaning of the master's qualification of
the labor-cost law, serves but to prove the assertion already

[1] P. 104.

made, that Ricardo's round-about argument on this subject was most misleading. As for Mr. Mill, his treatment of the interest difficulty was a bungle from first to last.

3. TORRENS.

5. Torrens explains at great length why commodities cannot be exchanged in primitive society on any other basis than that of labor cost; but concludes that the forces which produce this result in early times cause products to exchange, under advanced conditions, according to their capital cost. A commodity's cost in capital, measured as the money outlay of the capitalist-employer, is its "natural price." Actual exchange value does not, as Ricardo and Malthus say, tend to settle at *natural price,* because there is a permanent difference between these quantities, and this difference constitutes "profits." [1] It is true that writers who claim that the actual price tends to come to the "natural price" include profits in natural price,

"But this classification is highly unphilisophical and incorrect." [2] "We cannot assert that the profit of stock is included in the cost of production, without affirming the gross absurdity that the excess of value above the expenditure, constitutes a part of expenditure." [3]

The difference of view between Malthus and Torrens is easily explained. Malthus means by natural price, normal value. Torrens has in mind one variety of the "natural price" of the "philosophical" account of value.

"Natural price is that which we must give in order to obtain the article we want from the great warehouse of nature, and is the same thing as cost of production." [4]

[1] *Essay on the Production of Wealth*, London, 1821, p. 51. Torrens considered his theory of "exchangeable value" quite original, (Preface, p. 7.)

[2] P. 51. [3] P. 53. [4] P. 50.

In primitive times this was labor; in present times it is capital.

Torrens really attempted an "empirical" law,[1] namely, that the exchange values of commodities are *determined by* their cost in capital to the entrepreneur, but are in excess of the cost by a constant percentage. Exchange values are still determined by the cost, because the percentage of this excess is reckoned on the cost. In criticism of this, it is easy to show that, as an empirical account, the only possible way of defining entrepreneur's cost to show that it does regulate value is to include interest ("profits") in the cost. The "philosophical" account is brought to bear on the law of entrepreneur's costs only to injure its statement. Interest is a part of the cost of any particular commodity, in the sense that it must be paid to call forth capital to aid in its production, just as wages must be paid to call forth labor. If interest be excluded from entrepreneur's costs, the statement of Torrens that the value of the product will still be in proportion to cost cannot bear the slightest examination. The total process of the production of most goods is conducted by a series of entrepreneurs. If we take any two commodities of equal market value, the briefest consideration will show that their costs of production (in the sense employed by Torrens), merely to the last entrepreneur making them, may be quite unequal. As Ricardo pointed out, if one commodity takes longer to market after the entrepreneur makes his outlay than another, the amount of profits which its market value must afford will be greater, so that its cost (as Torrens defines it) must be less. But considering the entire cost of production to the series of entrepreneurs, the "profits" of each entrepreneur increase

---

[1] "Empirical," in the particular sense of this term, adopted in the opening chapter of this essay.

the necessary money outlay of the next entrepreneur succeeding him, who uses the product of the first as production goods. If Torrens should permit the profits of entrepreneurs earlier in the series surreptitiously to be included in the cost to later entrepreneurs, he would be abandoning his definition of cost. But if he excludes this element of profits to the whole series from the cost to the whole series, it is not true (for the same reason which applied to the case of the single entrepreneurs) that the values would be in proportion to costs of production.

6. Unfortunately, the influence of the philosophical account upon the thought of Torrens did not exhaust itself in the havoc it played with his theory of entrepreneur's cost. Perforce, he must give a new version of the theory of labor cost intended to bring it into complete harmony with the empirical law of costs. This theory is:

" it is always the amount of capital, or *quantity of accumulated labour*, and not the sum of accumulated and immediate labour expended on production, which determines the exchangeable value of commodities." [1]

No definition is given of " accumulated labor " other than that implied in the sentence above: " the amount of capital, *or* accumulated labour." Torrens defines capital to be the raw-material, machinery, and *subsistence of labor* necessary to production. The " accumulated labor " which a product costs must be, in his view, the labor [2] which its raw-material costs, plus that which the machinery used up for it costs,

---

[1] Pp. 39-40. See also Preface, p. 7. This theory does not occupy a prominent place in his book. The sum of accumulated and immediate labor is what Ricardo considers to be the total labor cost of a good—under the name of labor indirectly and directly applied.

[2] Presumably, in its turn, " *accumulated.*"

plus—*not* the labor actually employed on it in connection with this machinery, but plus the labor which the *subsistence* of this labor has *cost!* [1]

Since Torrens himself offers no explanation why this newly-defined quantity of labor cost should regulate value, we are not in duty bound to go very far into his fantastic conception. Just as labor theorists generally proved that labor cost is the regulator of value by the simple process of showing that utility is not, so, I suppose, Torrens shows that labor cost, as he defines it, regulates value because as defined by Ricardo it does not. An astonishing thing about his conception is that the labor *directly applied* to a thing is not a part of its labor cost! To the money outlay of the capitalist-entrepreneur for machinery and for raw-material corresponds the labor cost of these goods. To the money outlay in wages must correspond either the labor cost directly remunerated by these wages, *or else* the labor cost of the things the laborers buy with their money wages (subsistence). Both of these cannot be represented by these wages, otherwise some labor cost would be counted twice over. For instance, the labor employed directly on a pair of shoes would be part of the labor cost of production of the shoes; but somewhere else it would be counting as the cost of production of hats, or what not, according to the employment of the laborer of whose subsistence these shoes became a part. Having made the absurd choice to count this labor (the direct labor cost of the shoes) as part of the cost of hats, upon the general principle thus adopted, Torrens cannot count labor, directly applied, as part of the cost of the thing to which it is applied. From this it follows that the direct labor cost of a machine or a piece of raw-material cannot be counted as a part of the real labor cost which de-

---

[1] Explanation of this follows shortly.

termines its value.   As a consequence, it is interesting to note that none of the labor directly applied to a commodity, or directly applied to any production goods used up in it, is a part of its labor cost.   If Mr. Torrens had been pressed by a critic in his day, he could well have defied any man to locate the Torrens labor cost of an article to show that it *does not* correspond to the value of the article.

CHAPTER VII

THE EMPIRICAL THEORY AS DEVELOPED BY MALTHUS.

1. MALTHUS was a prolific and inconsistent writer on the subject of value.[1] His statement of the " empirical " laws of value was able, and materially advanced the theory in English political economy, but when he comes to the problem of the *measure of value,* as a part of what we call the philosophical account, his writings are of so little worth that it would be a waste of time to consider them in full. He was a great temporizer and user of makeshifts in questions of principle. Malthus denied the validity of Ricardo's labor-cost *regulator,* but defended the labor-command *measure,* which in turn Ricardo rejected. He had a direct correspondence controversy with the latter on the subject of these two standards, but what we have left of this correspondence is in many places almost unintelligible to a modern student, unless read with infinite care.[2]

2. In his *Principles,* Malthus opens his discussion by drawing the established distinction between value in use and value in exchange; but immediately after this he makes an

---

[1] In his *Principles,* 1st ed., 1820, and 2d ed., 1836, which was considerably altered from the first. *The Measure of Value Stated and Illustrated,* a pamphlet of 1823, and the *Definitions in Political Economy* may be mentioned, but the text of the two editions of the *Principles* suffices for any except the most minute investigation of his views.

[2] Ricardo's part is contained in his published letters to Malthus, as well as those to McCulloch and Trower, but the letters of Malthus to Ricardo have not, to my knowledge, been found for publication, except one given in *Letters of Ricardo to McCulloch,* (*Pub. Am. Ec. Assn.,* 10, Nos. 5–6) p. 161.

important alteration in the order of presentation of ideas, as followed by Smith and Ricardo. He begins with the "empirical" account of value. In consequence, when he turns to the question of the relation between labor cost and value, he is led to adjust the labor theory to the previously developed empirical theory. As pointed out in the introductory chapter of this essay, this was the beginning of the process which has resulted in the pushing aside of the labor theory in English political economy. Ricardo had been led, with injurious results, to adjust the "empirical" to the "philosophical" account.

In a history of the law of supply and demand, or of the law of entrepreneur's costs, the statement Malthus gave these principles would be of great importance.[1] Here we are concerned with his version of these principles only to the extent necessary to show the different *setting* they give the labor theory from that in Ricardo's work.

3. We find that in the view of Malthus, the primary principle of exchange value, or the principle of broadest application, is the law of supply and demand. The law of entrepreneur's costs is a secondary principle.

"It has never been a matter of doubt that the principle of supply and demand determines exclusively, and very regularly and accurately, the prices of monopolized commodities, without any reference to the cost of their production; and our daily and uniform experience shows us that the prices of raw products, particularly of those which are most affected by the seasons, are at the moment of their sale determined always

[1] The law of supply and demand is not so simple as to preclude a variety of ways of stating it, and the meaning of such conceptions as *intensity of demand, equilibrium* or *balance* of supply and demand, *etc.*, requires careful reasoning to define. The history of the law in English political economy would be concerned mainly with Malthus, J. S. Mill, Cairnes and Marshall.

by the higgling of the market, and differ widely in different years and at different times, while the labour and capital employed on them may have been very nearly the same." [1]

And even in those competitive manufactures where conditions are most favorable to the law of costs, alterations of the demand and supply are constantly overcoming the influence of cost. Therefore, the cost rule is not only limited in action, but it is directly subordinate to the rule of supply and demand.

"The cost of production itself only influences the price of * * commodities as the payment of this cost is the necessary condition of their continued supply."

"It follows that the great principle of demand and supply is called into action to determine what Adam Smith calls natural prices as well as market prices." [2]

Cost of production "can do nothing but in subordination" to the principle of supply and demand. [3]

Malthus follows Smith precisely in naming the components of entrepreneur's costs—wages, profits and rent—but prefers to call the normal value requisite to cover these expenses, instead of natural price, the *"necessary price,"* "because the term necessary better expresses a reference to the conditions of supply." [4] What he means by the statement that the relation of supply to demand not only determines temporary market prices but also natural prices as defined by Adam Smith, is that wages of labor depend on the supply of labor, and the "profits" of capital and rent of land

[1] *Principles*, 1st ed., pp. 73-4.
[2] *Ibid.*, 74-5.   [3] *Ibid.*, 76.
[4] *Ibid.*, p. 83.

in the same way on the supplies of these agents.[1] Ricardo took an entirely different view of the relation of the two "empirical" principles. In his work he takes no account of the law of supply and demand until in Chapter XXX, where he admits that this rule holds good of monopolized commodities, and, indeed, of all other commodities for a limited period.[2] But, in a letter to Malthus, he wrote:

"You say that demand and supply regulates (sic) value; this I think is saying nothing; it is supply which regulates value, and supply is itself controlled by comparative cost of production."[3]

Of course Ricardo was always conscious of the fact that cost of production can influence exchange value only by way of influencing supply. At the very outset of his chapter on value in his *Principles* he states:

"There are some commodities, the value of which is determined by their scarcity alone. No labour can increase the quantity

---

[1] The claim regarding the subordination of the law of costs is set forth emphatically as follows: "If it appears generally that the cost of production only determines the prices of commodities, as the payment of it is the necessary condition of their supply, and that the component parts of this cost are themselves determined [*i. e.*, as values] by the same causes which determine the whole, it is obvious that we cannot get rid of the principle of demand and supply by referring to the cost of production. Natural and necessary prices appear to be regulated by this principle, as well as market prices, and the only difference is that the former are regulated by the ordinary and average relation of the demand to the supply, and the latter when they differ from the former depend upon the extraordinary and accidental relations of the demand to the supply." *Principles*, 1st ed., pp. 84-85.

[2] Gonner ed., p. 376.

[3] *Letters to Malthus*, p. 176. Malthus's contrary opinion is defended at length by him in Sec. 11 of Chap. xi, on value, in the *Principles*, 1st ed.

of such goods, and therefore *their value cannot be lowered by an increased supply."* [1]

Ricardo's view was virtually this: The rule of supply and demand tells us practically nothing, but in those cases where we cannot get a further principle we will let it count as a law of value. But wherever the law of labor cost applies, the principle of supply and demand ceases to be of importance.

An attempt to determine whether Ricardo or Malthus was right would involve us immediately in a discussion of the ultimate relation of cost in all its forms to value, which, so far as we do enter into it, we hope to make the culmination of this essay. Which view is the more profound, and whether an ambiguity in the word value is involved in the controversy, are questions by no means easy to answer.

4. With this general theory, that the empirical law of costs is " subordinate " to the law of supply and demand, as a starting-point, Malthus proceeds to a thorough criticism of Ricardo's law of labor cost. In the indictment which he brings against this principle, we may for ourselves distinguish seven counts (indicated by the numbers in brackets). These counts really fall into two classes. The first main contention is that Ricardo considers the relation between entrepreneur's cost (" necessary price," as Malthus calls it; " natural price," or cost in " labour and profits," as Ricardo calls it) and actual market values too intimate. There are three sources of variation of actual from natural prices which should be emphasized. There are [1] the temporary market alterations of prices, too rapid to be met by changing the volume of production; [2] monopoly in the product itself, or some raw product used in its making; [3] seasonal fluctuations in all products of the soil.

[1] Gonner ed., p. 6. The same thought is expressed in the first paragraph of Chapter xiii, p. 171.

The second main contention [1] is that Ricardo overestimates the degree of control exercised by labor cost over natural price. Note the following comprehensive passage:

" Under all the variations, therefore, which arise [4] from the different proportions of fixed capital employed, the different quickness of the returns of the circulating capital, [5] the quantity of foreign commodities used in manufactures, [6] the acknowledged effects of taxation, [7] and the almost universal prevalence of rent in the actual state of all improved countries, we must I think allow that　＊　＊　＊　*it is certainly not* the quantity of labour which has been employed in the production of each particular commodity which determines their relative values in exchange at the same time and at the same place." [2]

The claim is in unequivocal language that " well-known causes of constant and universal operation " destroy the proportionality of value to labor cost.

It will be observed that the four points made in this citation all concern influences which make the entrepreneur's expenses of production out of proportion to the total quantity of labor which his outlay of money directly and indirectly remunerates. For instance, the fifth point regarding the use of imported raw-material or machinery refers to the fact that $1,000 worth of production goods bought abroad by an entrepreneur may have cost more or less labor than $1,000 worth of raw-material of home production. As Ricardo himself points out (in Chapter VII of his *Principles*), the exchange value of an imported commodity does

---

[1] The case is not presented by Malthus as one of two main arguments with seven counts in total, but all except this division and the numbering are his.

[2] 1st ed., pp. 104-5. This passage happens not to reappear in the 2d ed., but all the points in it are still maintained there.

not depend on its labor cost abroad compared with the home labor cost of the goods against which it exchanges. But the $1,000 spent by one entrepreneur counts just the same as that spent by another in determining the " necessary price " of the respective commodities which they produce. Thus there is here one source of disproportionality between necessary prices and actual labor costs.

5. What is the position of Ricardo with respect to these seven counts? He acknowledged all but the claim that rent causes an aberration of normal value from the position required by labor cost. That is, in the language of the day he denied that " rent enters into price." He not only acknowledged, but himself stated the other points. How fully he treats the question of the different proportions of " fixed and circulating " capital, we have seen.[1] As for the " acknowledged " effects of taxation, the reference is to Ricardo's own statements, scattered throughout his various chapters on taxation, that this and that tax will raise prices. Ricardo was perfectly aware of the effects of monopoly, and of the influence of temporary oscillations of supply and demand.[2]

[1] As Malthus said in another place, "The effects of slow or quick returns, and of the different proportions of fixed and circulating capitals, are distinctly allowed by Mr. Ricardo, but in his last edition he has much underrated their amount. They are both theoretically and practically so considerable as entirely to destroy the position that commodities exchange with each other according to the quantity of labour which has been employed upon them, but no one that I am aware of has ever stated that the different quantity of labour employed on commodities is not a much more powerful source of difference of value." *Measure of Value Stated and Illustrated*, pp. 12–13.

[2] We have not happened upon a passage by Ricardo referring to the third count, respecting good and bad crops, but Ricardo would undoubtedly have considered that it did not invalidate his position. If agricultural capital and labor remain the same in quantity while good and bad crops alternate, the *cost of production per unit of crop* varies as well as the price. When the wheat crop is good the cost per

The old question whether " rent enters into price " could very properly be discussed in a history of the labor theory of value. Since, however, the question is large enough to warrant separate discussion, and has in recent times received it in many prominent places, we shall be content merely to point out the conflict between Malthus and Ricardo, and to take the stand that recent discussion has shown that ground rent enters into price in the same sense as wages, or interest on capital other than land. Ricardo said rent does not and cannot enter in the least degree into price. Says Malthus:

" It appears to me essential, both to correctness of language and correctness of meaning to say that the cost of producing any commodity is made up of all the wages, all the profits, and all the rent which   *   *   are necessary to bring that particular commodity to market in the quantity required." [1]

6. We have here the remarkable instance of two writers nearly agreed on the number of exceptions to a principle, but quite disagreed as to what remains of the principle. The labor cost of a commodity in a modern market can influence its exchange value only by means of influencing its entrepreneur's cost. Thus any cause which weakens the connection between the value of a commodity and its entrepreneur's cost of production, thereby also weakens its connection with labor cost. Therefore, the first three points made by Malthus to show that entrepreneur's costs do not exercise perfect control over actual market-values are relevant

bushel is low. The price per bushel would also be low. If good crops mean low cost and low value at the same time, they probably do not mean sinking of value and cost in the same degree. The consequent deviation of value from cost is probably what Malthus had in mind.

[1] 1st ed., pp. 102-3.

to the dispute about the labor-cost regulator. But, as the reader has observed, the three exceptions to the law of money costs are only such as have always been made to any proposition of static theory. A static law of value is supposed only to govern *normal value* under competitive conditions. It is perfectly legitimate to put emphasis upon the causes of the variation of actual values from static standards, but on the principle, now so well understood, that actual conditions can be fully understood only by the preliminary establishment of static laws, the first three points of criticism made by Malthus, and admitted by Ricardo, must be judged to leave the law of costs a perfectly valid principle.

If the only causes of variation of actual exchange values from the standard of labor costs were those causes which operate to weaken the law of entrepreneur's costs, the Ricardian labor theory would remain a principle of the utmost importance. The attacks which the labor-cost theory cannot withstand are those directed against its validity *as a static principle.* It is an undisputed static principle that exchange values are in proportion to entrepreneur's costs. Therefore, every time a cause is shown which throws entrepreneur's costs out of proportion to labor cost, a heart-thrust is given the theory of the labor-cost regulator. To the list of causes of this kind granted by Ricardo, Malthus added one, an important one; or rather, he persisted in retaining what Adam Smith considered to be such a cause— rent of land. Malthus then discovered no new point; but he marshaled many points in an able manner. Considering only the weighty part of his case, his argument is that entrepreneur's costs consist of wages, interest, and rent; that wages alone stand for labor cost; [1] that therefore the exist-

[1] The strange attempt of James Mill to show that the interest element stands for labor also, mistook, as we showed in Chapter vi, the replacement fund of an entrepreneur for his interest fund.

ence of the other two elements makes the total entrepreneur's cost decidedly out of proportion to labor cost. This signifies not only that entrepreneur's costs are composed of outlays in excess of payments for labor, but that when one entrepreneur's cost is compared with that of another the two will (barring an accidental coincidence) not be to each other as the respective labor costs entering into them (through wages). Two commodities may have equal exchange values and equal entrepreneur's costs, but one may cost twice as much labor as the other, because the latter may cost more rent or interest than the former. Ricardo denied the influence of rent, and *assumed* that interest preserves fairly constant proportions with the wage element. In our judgment, Ricardo was much the profounder of these two economists, but Malthus made the fortunate gain of presenting the empirical principles of value at the outset of his work, and in this way was led to adjust the labor theory to them, instead of doing the reverse, as Ricardo did.

Note on the Question of the Invariable Measure of Value in all Times and Places.

7. Adam Smith made several general assertions concerning the power of a labor standard to measure value *in all times and places.* If mankind should live under conditions free from the rent of land and interest on capital, according to Smith the quantity of labor which commodities cost might properly be regarded as commensurate with the quantity which they command in exchange. Under actual conditions the command standard alone will apply. Ricardo became a steadfast critic of the idea that the labor-command standard could be thus used. He believed it to be impossible to find an invariable measure based on labor cost of production (as distinguished from labor commanded in exchange) ; but he made statements which implied that if a commodity existed which cost the same quantity of labor throughout time, it would

be an invariable measure of " real value." Then again he faltered in this view because " profits " enter into the cost of production of different articles in different degrees. The writer has found himself unable to reach a complete understanding of Ricardo's section on this subject, Section vi of Chapter 1. Malthus always defended the labor-command standard of Smith, though in a vacillating way. In the end he adopted it in an unqualified form. (In the 2d and last edition of his *Principles,* the text being written just before his death.) With his last published discussion, appearing in 1836, the question practically disappeared from English political economy. Referring to this question, John Stuart Mill said : "it is necessary to touch upon the subject, if only to show how little there is to be said about it," and concludes that the measure sought is impossible. J. B. Say wrote that " an invariable measure of value is a pure Chimera." [1]   Torrens expressed his judgment in words quoted from Lord Lauderdale : " Lord Lauderdale has justly observed that the search of economists after a measure of exchangeable value, is just as irrational and as hopeless as was that of the alchemists in quest of the philosopher's stone." [2]   Well might the discussion be condemned by contemporaries and neglected by subsequent economists, for, especially in the lengthy writings of Malthus, the question was involved in distracting confusion, while the comparatively brief passage Smith devoted to the subject contains fatal contradictions.

It is doubtful if we can escape this question in theory. The required standard may come as a more modest proposal than that of Adam Smith, but some means of comparing value, as significance (as Menger's *"Bedeutung"*) in different times will always be desirable, to say the least. In the recent controversy over the question whether gold is a good standard of de-

[1] In his notes in a French edition of Ricardo's *Principles,* " *Des Principes de l' Economie Politique et de l'Impôt,*" 2d ed. Paris (1835), note, p. 12.

[2] *Essay on the Production of Wealth,* p. 65.

ferred payments, practical men decided for gold on other (and sufficient) grounds than any alleged invariability in value, but it was inevitable that the question should suggest itself: What does constitute the same *value* in different times (*i. e.* under changed conditions of wealth)?   It is the legitimate function of economic theory to wrestle with such questions, whether to conclude that an answer is impossible (for that would be a conclusion, hard to prove and of importance when proved) or that such and such a standard may be established.

The present essay will not attempt the herculean dialectical labor of setting in order and criticising all that Smith, Malthus, and Ricardo wrote on this subject.   The labor doctrine as a statical theory is a problem of sufficient proportions in itself to permit specializing upon it.   A brief discussion however is added concerning what Malthus wrote upon the subject of the labor-command measure.   In the first edition of his *Principles,* Malthus held that there is no question of possessing a perfect measure of value at different times, but there is a question of choice between various imperfect measures.   He was apparently much impressed by the charge that the value of labor changes when the quantity of commodity (*i. e.* measured in physical units) which it commands, is altered.   Accordingly he proposes to take labor and "corn" together, or a "mean between them" as a standard.[1]   He proceeds upon the supposition that " when corn compared with labour is dear, labour compared with corn must necessarily be cheap. "At the period when a given quantity of corn will command the greatest quantity of the necessaries, conveniences, and amusements of life, a given quantity of labour will always command the smallest quantity of such objects, (and *vice versa*) ;   *   *   *   If, then, we take a mean between the two, we shall evidently have a measure corrected by the contemporary variations of each in opposite directions." [2]

[1] The principle of this choice had very little in common with the principle of the various " multiple standards of value " since proposed.

[2] 1st ed., pp. 128-9.

In this double standard a unit of labor is to be a *day* of " common " labor. For the use of the standard some unit of corn is necessary. A *peck* is selected. The reason given for this choice is that this amount may be considered " in respect to quantity as equivalent to a day's labour." Accordingly, " any commodity, which at different periods will purchase the same number of days' labour and of pecks of wheat, or parts of them, each taken in equal proportions, may be considered, upon this principle, as commanding pretty nearly the same quantity of the necessaries, conveniences, and amusements of life; and, consequently, as preserving pretty nearly its real value in exchange at different periods." [1] In his correspondence with Malthus, Ricardo made the former very uncomfortable in the position taken with respect to the combined labor-corn measure of value. In the second edition of the *Principles* of Malthus this hybrid standard was abandoned. In principle it was a shallow makeshift. It is needless to say that if the arguments for regarding the amount of commodities purchaseable by a day's wages, as the unit of wealth, are sufficient, grain should be measured in its " real value " by reference to this standard in the same way as any other important commodity. As was stated in Chapter ii, the corn measure of value was suggested by Smith to serve as a convenient index to the labor measure. Beyond a doubt, Smith spoke of the corn measure in a way to mislead both Ricardo and Malthus; but nothing could be plainer than the words quoted from him to show that corn is used on principle only because it is supposed to remain from age to age in a steady exchange ratio with day labor. [2]

In Malthus's second edition, the view is taken simply that " standard " labor commanded in exchange is the measure of value in all times and places. There is great difficulty in telling precisely what value, or what kind of value, it is that is measured. It is called " real value in exchange " and " in-

[1] 1st ed., p. 129.   [2] See ante, p. 27, n.

trinsic value in exchange." The latter is in one place defined
to be "not the general power of purchasing possessed by a
particular commodity, but its power of purchasing *arising from
intrinsic causes,* which includes all the causes of whatever
kind they may be, which have contributed to the limitation of its supply compared with the demand." [1] The extrinsic causes of a commodity's exchange value are the
causes of the value of the other commodity in whose
quantity the exchange value of the first is expressed. [2] In
various other places, "intrinsic value in exchange" is defined as indicating (1) the degree of necessity or convenience to
life (1st ed.) ; (2) the difficulty of obtainment (in some sense
supposed to be more inclusive than Ricardo's labor cost) ;
(3) the degree of the limitation of the supply as compared
with the demand. Thinking with such terminology would be
like painting portraits with a white-wash brush. If a day of
labor in America commanded twice the physical quantity of
a given complex of commodities that a day of English labor
commanded, Malthus was forced to admit that the simple exchange value of the goods commanded by a unit of American
labor was twice that commanded by a unit of British labor.
But at the same time his doctrine of the labor measure of value
required him to affirm that the "real exchange value" of the
goods commanded by a day of labor in the two countries was
the same. In this way he was led to contend that two com-
plexes of goods having different exchange values, had the
same "real exchange values." In view of the fact that "real
exchange value" is defined virtually as "exchange value as
arising from its causes," the contention is mystifying. One
is prone to acquiesce in J. S. Mill's judgment that the argument of Malthus is a "vain subtlety."

[1] 2d ed., p. 96.   [2] 2d ed., p. 57.

CHAPTER VIII

SENIOR

1. SENIOR's little *Political Economy* [1] earned for him but a secondary rank in the literary history of the science. This is because the work, taken as a whole, is extremely unsystematic. It is also a little erratic. Senior was, however, a man of far greater merit than McCulloch, Torrens, or James Mill, and advanced many significant original doctrines, or rather parts of doctrines. The most noteworthy of these bear closely upon the theory of value; and if we put together what he said, in our own way, we shall obtain an important line of commentary upon the Ricardian labor-cost theory. The results tend more to destroy than to support that theory. [2]

According to Senior, the conditions essential to value, which he defines as exchange value, are (1) utility, (2) limitation in supply, (3) transferableness. [3] We have seen

---

[1] Prepared as the article on "Political Economy" in the *Encyclopædia Metropolitana*, 1836, but appearing as a separate work in numerous reprints from this. Page references are good for any edition. The table of contents looks systematic at first blush, but study of the text, especially the part on the theory of distribution, soon dispels any illusions concerning this point.

[2] Senior was, in my judgment, indebted fully as much to Malthus and Say as to Ricardo. To all appearances much of interest in the writings of Cairnes must have been suggested by the work of Senior.

[3] *Political Economy*, p. 6. These are the three constituents of *wealth*, but things composing wealth are defined to be the same as things of value. Curiously the qualification of transferableness is held not to exclude per-

how Malthus laid emphasis on the fact that cost can influence value only through affecting supply, and here we see the same thought put even more emphatically. It is *limitation of supply* alone that in the first instance gives value to things of a useful nature. The following words, carrying out the lines of thought suggested by J. B. Say and Malthus, are remarkable:

" It is true that wherever there is utility, the addition of labor as necessary to production constitutes value, because, the supply of labor being limited, it follows that the object to the supply of which it is necessary, is by that very necessity limited in supply. But any other cause limiting supply is just as efficient a cause of value in an article as the necessity of labor to its production. And in fact, if all the commodities used by man were supplied by nature without any intervention whatever of human labor, but were supplied in precisely the same quantities as they now are, there is no reason to suppose either that they would cease to be valuable, or would exchange in any other than their present proportions." [1]

Senior adopts this last heroic hypothesis only in passing, by way of exhibiting, in a striking way, what he considers to be the true relation of labor cost to value. In criticism of Ricardo, he says:

"As limitation of supply is essential to the value of labor itself, to assume labor and exclude limitation of supply, as the condition on which value depends is not only to substitute a partial for a general cause, but pointedly to exclude the very cause which gives force to the cause assigned."

sonal talents from the category of wealth, for these are considered to be things "imperfectly transferable." A lawyer transfers his talents to me when I hire him to plead my case. See pp. 9–10.

[1] P. 24. A similar passage, not so well expressed, is found in Malthus, *Principles*, 1st ed., p. 74.

2. Although Senior is careful to give limitation of supply as the factor which, combined with usefulness, occasions value, he still holds that cost of production may govern value under certain ideal conditions. These conditions are described as those of " perfect competition," but he means a great deal more by this than these words signify to-day. Senior's conception of cost, however, is different from Ricardo's. " By *cost of production* we mean the sum of labour and abstinence necessary to production." [1] Labor is defined, with especial reference to cutting off the extension of the term attempted by McCulloch,[2] to be " voluntary exertion of bodily or mental faculties for the purposes of production " (p. 57). The new word *abstinence* is defined as follows:

"A term by which we express the conduct of a person who either abstains from the unproductive use of what he can command, or designedly prefers the production of remote to that of immediate results." [3]

For the variety of conceptions of cost, expressed and implied in the writings of his predecessors, Senior substitutes a consistent definition of cost in terms of subjective sacrifice. With this improved concept as an aid, he is enabled to resolve many of the difficulties which had beset earlier debates upon the meaning of cost. The objection of Mr. Torrens to the inclusion by Mr. Malthus of " profits " in cost is good, says Senior, as against Mr. Malthus's word *profits*.

[1] P. 101.

[2] See *ante*, chap. vi, § 2.

[3] P. 58. Scrope, an English writer, 1833, said: "Profit is to be viewed in the light of a compensation for abstaining for a time from consumption in personal gratification." Mentioned by Böhm-Bawerk, *Capital and Interest*, p. 271. "But," continues Böhm-Bawerk, "this same idea which his predecessors merely touched on, Senior has made the center of a well-constructed theory of interest."

" Want of the term abstinence, or of some equivalent expression has led Mr. Malthus into inaccuracy of language. * *
When he termed profit a part of the cost of production, he appears to us to have meant not profit, but that conduct which is repaid by profit: an inaccuracy precisely similar to that committed by those who term wages a part of the cost of production; meaning not wages, which are the result, but the labour for which wages are the remuneration." [1]

The clearness of thought here is gratifying in comparison with earlier discussions, but, as we have had occasion to urge before, the idea that it is erroneous to consider wages and profits as cost, confines the term to the meaning of subjective cost whereas there can well be other forms of cost. It may cost coal and machinery to produce an article, just as it may cost labor and abstinence.

3. The true cost of production of commodities, affirms Senior, would regulate their values if the only obstacles to their supply were the labor and abstinence required for their production.   There are two different arguments given to substantiate this proposition.   The first partially corresponds to the " philosophical " account of value, being stated in highly generalized terms without regard to the division of society into classes of capitalists and laborers.

" Where the only natural agents employed are those which are universally accessible, and therefore are practically unlimited in supply, the utility of the produce, or in other words, its power of producing gratification, or preventing pain, must be in proportion to the sacrifices made to produce it, unless the producer has misapplied his exertions: *Since* no man would willingly employ a given amount of labor or abstinence in producing one commodity, if he could obtain more gratification by devoting them to the production of another." [2]

[1] P. 100.   [2] P. 97.

This passage, whether consciously or unconsciously, is a proposition about a primitive or a Robinson Crusoe economy. It affirms that the utility of products will be *in proportion to* their total disutility costs of production, but it does not affirm that production will be carried on until the utility per unit of the increasing number of products will be reduced until it is *equal to* the disutility cost of a unit. Except for the failure to make this latter observation, Senior's formula looks like an anticipation of later theories of value. This appearance is carried out by the use of the word "utility" for value. The word as here used was probably taken directly from Say; it cannot be Adam Smith's "*value in use.*" For if Crusoe produced at equal cost, measured in disutility, a small article of luxury and a great quantity of necessaries, and estimated the two at the same value—and this would be normal—the Smithian values in use distinctly would not be in proportion to sacrifice costs. The great quantity of necessaries would have a great "value in use," as contrasted with the small article of luxury, for which Crusoe nevertheless was willing to expend quite as much labor. "Marginal" or "final" utility would fit the requirements of this formula, but there is nowhere in the book the slightest evidence that Senior utilizes the marginal method. In fact, on the same page with this proposition is a paragraph which shows that he considers the value of things not capable of increase in supply—the "rare productions of nature and art"—to be subject to no general rule, because dependent merely on the wealth and taste of the community.[1] That is to say, unless there is some ascertainable rule governing the conditions of the supply of goods, there is no rule of their value. But the utility

[1] P. 97. *Cf.* p. 105.

theory is a whole explanation of value lying precisely in this region of no rules.[1]

4. We come shortly to the explanation that nearly corresponds with Adam Smith's " empirical account." Here the scene is the social economy. Cost of production—always the sum of labor and abstinence—must be divided into (a) cost on the part of the producer or seller and (b) on the part of the consumer or purchaser. The latter is the amount of labor and abstinence which would have to be undergone by the consumers if they themselves, or some of them in behalf of themselves and the others, were to resort to producing the good in question instead of buying it. The former cost sets the minimum limit to price, or exchange value. The latter sets the maximum. Under circumstances of free competition, when no producer possesses any advantage over another, these two limits coincide, and the price of commodities therefore represents the aggregate amount of labor and abstinence necessary to continue their production.[2] This division of cost into two parts, each forming a limit, is Senior's peculiar and inferior way of describing the action of competition among producers. He concludes nearly in the ordinary way:

" If the price should rise beyond the cost of their [the commodities'] production, the producers must receive more than an average remuneration for their sacrifices. As soon as this has been discovered capital and industry flow towards the employment which, by this supposition, offers extraordinary advantages. Those who formerly were purchasers, or persons on their behalf, turn producers themselves, until the increased supply has equalized the price with the cost of production." [3]

The reverse movement, of course, prevents an abnormal fall

[1] But yet of all English writers previous to Jevons, he develops the explanation most compatible with the utility theory of value.

[2] P. 101.   [3] P. 101.

of prices. This process of bringing exchange values into proportion to subjective costs of production, reduces itself simply to the adjustment of values to such a level that the wages and profits into which they are divided in each industry furnish the regular or average (as we should say, " static ") remuneration to the labor and abstinence required for production.

5. We see, then, that where labor and abstinence are the only " obstacles " to supply, or where profits and wages are the only shares which " enter into " price, values will be in proportion to cost of production, which is not labor, but a " sum of labor and abstinence." The next question is, in what light does Senior regard *rent*. Rent, in his view, overturns the whole correlation of value with subjective cost of production. And here we are introduced to Senior's remarkable extension of the concepts of *rent* and of *natural agents*. In the first place, rent is defined to be the return to natural agents which are not universally accessible (p. 90). But in the second place, rent is defined to be the surplus of value produced above the amount required to remunerate the sacrifices of production.

" If the established division is adhered to, and all that is produced is to be divided into rent, profit, and wages,—and certainly that appears to be the most convenient classification,— and if wages and profit are to be considered as the rewards of peculiar sacrifices, * * * it is clear that under the term ' rent ' must be included all that is obtained without any sacrifice; or, which is the same thing, beyond the remuneration for that sacrifice; all that nature or fortune bestows either without any exertion on the part of the recipient, or in addition to the average remuneration for the exercise of industry or the employment of capital." [1]

[1] Pp. 91-2. P. 128, the question of nomenclature is discussed all over again. Rent is "the revenue spontaneously offered by nature or accident."

Accordingly, rent includes not only the return to land, in the widest economic sense of this term, but also the return to secret processes of production, and to talents or extraordinary personal abilities.[1] This necessitates the very curious use of the words " natural agents " to include exclusive knowledge of, or right to, an advanced process, and talents or unusual faculties:

" The mere knowledge of the operations of nature, as long as the use of that knowledge can be confined either by secrecy or law, creates a revenue to its possessor analogous to the rent of land * * * so precisely resembling the rent of land, that it often receives the same name," (and it must be called rent).

The salary, wages, or remuneration of the laborer may really be composed of wages, rent, and profits:

" Is then the extraordinary remuneration of the labourers, which is assisted by extraordinary talents, to be termed Rent or Wages? It originates in the bounty of nature; so far it seems to be rent. It is to be obtained only on the condition of undergoing labour; so far it seems to be wages. It might be termed * * rent which can be received only by a labourer, or wages which can be received only by the proprietor of a natural agent. But as it is clearly a surplus, the labour having been previously paid for by average wages, and that surplus the spontaneous gift of nature, we have thought it most convenient to term it rent." [2]

---

[1] Pp. 91, 128–135. For general argument to justify inclusion of personal qualities within *wealth*, see pp. 9–10.

[2] *Ibid.*, pp. 129–30. Some of the extraordinary earning power or ability of the laborer may be the result of education and training for which sacrifices have been made. Such abilities are "*immaterial capital*," and the part of the whole wages due to them is really profit on this capital (p. 130). Then wages of skilled or professional labor may

6. Does this rent, the surplus of value above reward for true cost of production, " enter into price?" Senior does not use these words or discuss this question directly, but, although he follows Ricardo precisely in explaining rent as a differential return and defends the doctrine vigorously against Say's attacks, he assumes nevertheless, contrary to Ricardo, that rent does " enter into price " in the sense of constituting a source of permanent disproportionality of value to subjective cost of production. As was intimated some pages back, the state of free competition, as understood by Senior, is highly ideal, postulating not only the ordinary condition of ideal mobility of capital and labor, but also the use of none but free natural agents:

" When we speak, therefore, of a class of commodities as produced under circumstances of equal competition, or as the result of labour and abstinence unassisted by any other appropriated agent, * * * we do not mean to state that any such commodities exist, but that, if they did exist, such would be the laws by which their prices would be regulated." [1]

He takes up the example of the watch, a commodity adduced by McCulloch and others as having a value derived from labor cost alone, and shows that at every turn *rent,* of the diverse kinds he has defined, is paid out of its price.[2]

contain *rent* for inborn talents, *profit* for abilities acquired through the sacrifice called abstinence, and *wages* for the real disutility of labor incurred. "Forty pounds a year would probably pay all the labour that [a lawyer] undergoes in order to make, we will say, £4,000 a year. Of the remaining £3,960 probably £3,000 may be considered rent" (p. 134). "The intellectual and moral capital of Great Britain far exceeds all her material capital, not only in importance, but even in productiveness." *Ibid.*

[1] P. 114.

[2] P. 112. The payment of rent in every case is but the wedging in of a slice between value and the remuneration for cost of production.

7. What is the net result of Senior's argument for the labor-cost theory of value? In the first place, Senior had little to say about the difficulty of "fixed and circulating capital" which took so much of Ricardo's time. The reason is simple. Of course the values of products are out of proportion to their labor costs, because of the different lengths of time required to produce them. Two goods may cost the same labor, but differ in value.

"The principle is that, though in both cases the labour employed is the same, more abstinence is necessary in the one case than in the other." [1]

The great effort of Ricardo to force the facts into some conformity with the only philosophy of value he possessed, by asking us to consider "profits" an element about in proportion to wages cost, though they are not, becomes unnecessary from Senior's view-point. The motive to undertake this forcing of facts is undermined. For "profits" stand on the subjective basis of "abstinence," just as wages stand on the base of labor.

Furthermore, according to Senior, land rent "enters into" price. So far, both "profits" of stock and rent of land exist to destroy the proportionality of values to labor cost. This is the result to which Malthus's criticisms of Ricardo had led. But Senior's criticism goes beyond Malthus's. Wages, as an element in entrepreneur's cost, are not even in proportion to the labor remunerated. That is to say, this is what Senior says if we keep his thought while reforming his language. He states that the actual income, which we always call *wages,* is really composed in many cases of wages, profits, and rent. He says this because he wishes to define wages as that remuneration which is in proportion to sacrifice. In this departure in terminology we

[1] Pp. 100-101.

cannot follow him. It is the whole wage of a laborer which is truly analogous to the rent of a physical unit of land. Different laborers, of different earning capacities, could be conceived of as ranged in a scale, so as to give a differential aspect to their incomes. Senior's *rent to skill* is really *an excess of wages* over the amount required to be in proportion to disutility. As he himself wrote in one place:

" There are few employments in which extraordinary powers of body and mind do not receive an extraordinary remuneration. It is the privilege of talent to work not only better but *more easily.* It will generally be found, therefore, that the commodity or service produced by a first-rate workman, while it sells for more than an average price, has *cost less than an average amount of labor,* [*i. e.,* disutility.]" [1]

Said Ricardo: The principle of value is that labor cost regulates it; but this principle is considerably modified by the fact that the values of different commodities have to include different proportions of " profit." Piecing together for ourselves what Senior says, it is his position that the value of commodities must include (if the commodities are to be produced) rent, profits, and wages; rent and profits, being different percentages in the whole entrepreneur's cost of different goods, make values out of proportion to labor cost; there is no necessity of considering profits as an element in entrepreneur's costs approximately in proportion to wages; and lastly, wages are not in proportion to labor, which is disutility. [2]

[1] P. 129.

[2] In an unobtrusive position further on in the book he adopts the labor-command standard, but without discussion. " The best standard of value for philosophical purposes appears to be the command of labour." This appears to be an uncritical and passing acquiescence in the views of Malthus.

CHAPTER IX

JOHN STUART MILL

1. Though Mill regarded his exposition of the theory of value with great satisfaction—a fact that has occasioned innumerable thrusts at him since—his contributions to the whole subject were not great, considering the work of Ricardo, the criticisms of it by Malthus, and the abundance of suggestions in the writings of Senior. His terminological faults are gross, and in many places his thought is very loose. His entire discussion of value, above all, lacks precision. By value is to be understood exchange value, general power of purchasing, and Mill insists strongly on the necessity of keeping in mind that a general rise or fall of value so defined is "unthinkable." Value is purely a relative term. The conditions essential to value are utility and difficulty of attainment. Difficulty of attainment may " consist in an absolute limitation of supply " or in " the labour and expense requisite to produce the commodity." [1] When, in the latter event, labor is applied under conditions of diminishing returns, a third case of value is distinguished for separate treatment. Following Malthus in his important innovation of giving the " empirical account " precedence, Mill begins with the assertion that the law of

---

[1] *Principles*, 6th ed., vol. i, pp. 546-7. The language is uncritical. Absolute limitation of supply is not a case of difficulty of attainment, but a case of value apart from questions cf difficulty of attainment. Senior's analysis was superior.

value of the first class of things—namely, those under an absolute limitation of supply—is merely the law of supply and demand.

"There is another law for that much larger class of things which admit of indefinite multiplication." [1] This is a law of entrepreneur's costs of production. While demand and supply rule alone in a certain field, and rule over the oscillations of value in all fields, in the case of reproducible goods,

"they themselves [*i. e.* demand and supply] obey a superior force, which makes value gravitate towards Cost of Production. * * * Demand and Supply always rush to an equilibrium, but the condition of stable equilibrium is when things exchange for each other according to their cost of production." [2]

Cost is called now by Ricardo's words "natural value;" now by Malthus's, "necessary price." Cost of production is defined as follows, in the chapter which summarizes the theory of value:

"Cost of production consists of several elements, some of which are constant and universal, others occasional. The universal elements of cost of production are the wages of the labour and the profits of the capital. The occasional elements are, taxes and any extra cost occasioned by a scarcity value of some of the requisites."

With respect to rent, Mill follows Ricardo for the general rule, instead of Malthus and Senior:

"Rent is not an element in the cost of production of the commodity which yields it; except in the case (rather conceivable than actually existing) in which it results from, and represents, a scarcity value. But when land capable of yield-

[1] Vol. i, p. 552.   [2] Vol. i, p. 561.

ing rent in agriculture is applied to some other purpose, the rent which it would have yielded is an element in the cost of production of the commodity which it is employed to produce."[1]

If Mill had followed the lead given in the last sentence to its logical end, the result ought to have been the inclusion of ground-rent as an element in entrepreneur's costs. But, in spite of these concessions, he thought of rent habitually as failing to enter into price, and thus failing to be a cause of disproportionality between labor-cost and value.

2. The profit of capital is stated explicitly to be the remuneration of abstinence, but nothing is made to depend on this.[2] Abstinence is not elevated into a position logically coördinate with labor, nor are the two conceived of together as constituting subjective costs, as distinguished from entrepreneur's costs, consisting in profits and wages.[3] While the language of Mill in diverse places shows that he was well enough aware of the difference between the two main forms of cost, so little was this essential distinction ever ready in his mind that he is able to say, without realizing the offence, just as Ricardo does: "Besides the natural and necessary elements in cost of production—labour and profits * * "[4] When the time comes to develop the traditional philosophical account of value, abstinence is forgotten. Labor alone comes to the front. The aberration, due to profits, of the value of products from the standard required by labor cost, is treated not in a "philosophical" account like Senior's, which endeavors to include and explain the case, but is regarded as an exception to the "philosophical" explanation, or as an error in it.

---

[1] Vol. i, p. 589.   [2] Vol. i, p. 568.

[3] The socialists' attacks upon abstinence as a cost are really directed against the *ethical* coördination of it with labor.

[4] Vol. i, p. 574.

3. There is a place in his book where Mill wavers in the decision to include profits in cost of production. The probable explanation of his hesitancy is of considerable interest, for it suggests the internal weakness of the theory that cost in any form is the essence of value. His doubt arises in connection with the familiar case of the relative values of a cask of wine and a piece of cloth, originally costing the same amount of labor in their production. The difficulty arises from the fact that the wine alone continues to increase in value through mere lapse of time:

" The wine and the cloth were made by the same original outlay. Here then is a case in which the natural values, relatively to one another, of two commodities, do not conform to their cost of production alone, but to their cost of production plus something else."

In this sentence Mill excludes " profits " from cost. But he continues : " Unless, indeed, for the sake of generality in the expression, we include the profit which the wine merchant *foregoes* during the five years in the cost of production of the wine." [1] The word " foregoes " (not italicized by Mill) is uncalled for. The wine merchant does not get profits he foregoes elsewhere, but the profits he makes from the added value of the wine. They might be greater or less than the profits foregone elsewhere. The forces tending to make them equal to those elsewhere relinquished are precisely the same in this case as in any other. If they are greater, more five-year-old wine will be brought to the market and its price will fall, and if they are less the reverse will happen. What is the difference between this case and the case of an ordinary industrial product that Mill should falter so? Does capital (using the term in the

[1] Vol. i, pp. 569–70.

sense defined by J. B. Clark), the fund of wealth employed in production, play different rôles in the two cases? Not in the least. Suppose a fund of capital is embodied in a certain quantity of raw material for a certain length of time until the same becomes final product. The final product, besides covering all other expenses, affords a sum of value equal to the capital invested in materials plus the interest on it. The difficulty felt in the case of the wine was undoubtedly that no tools, machinery, or labor were employed upon it during the time of its improvement in value. The changes working within it effected its increase in value merely by augmenting its utility to users of wine. The increase of value, secondly, affords a " profit " or interest. This profit may strike the mind as a surplus over cost to the entrepreneur, but the relation of this interest to the value of the final product is precisely the same as in any common case of manufacture. Interest as a cost can influence the value of the product only by influencing its supply. To discover the essential nature of value, we must lay bare the causes which determine what the value of a given supply is, independently of its cost. Cost and value may, in certain cases, tend to make mutual adjustments, but these are effected only by means of changes in supply. Value is not determined by cost *per se,* or, that is to say, cost is by no means of its essence. In the ordinary case, if one capital is employed for a longer time than another, the outwardly active process of production is continued for a longer time. If extra profit accrues through a time when labor works and wheels turn, it is easy to say that profits must be paid, and therefore the value of the product must be of such and such an extent. But in an instance where the value increases without the whirl of wheels and the manipulation of tools, the phenomenon naturally presents itself to the mind in an unfamiliar aspect. The wine merchant remains passive, and it seems plain that instead of his expense dictating what the value of the wine shall be, the truth is, he takes what the causes independently determining the value of the wine give him. Beyond a doubt there is a relation of cost to value, but there are instances where the ultimate philosophy that cost is the very essence of value applies with such unsatisfactory results that any but the most doctrinaire classical economist must falter and hasten on.

4. If " profits " are a part of entrepreneur's cost of production, the question which confronted Ricardo must reappear. Does not the variety of the proportions in which fixed and circulating capital are combined in production, free values from the regulation of labor cost? The consideration of this question in Mill's *Principles* is accompanied by unpardonable blunders in terminology. Mill's mind seems here completely tradition-ridden. The havoc is wrought in the use of terms by adopting the view that besides labor cost influencing value, wages also influence it. In the topical analysis (Table of Contents, vol. i, p. 15) the outline of the chapter on cost of production proceeds as follows:

" Principal element in cost of production, quantity of labour. Wages not an element in cost of production, except in so far as they vary from employment to employment."

When cost is used in a sense which makes labor one of its elements, wages are not an element in so far as they vary from employment to employment, or in any other way. In the sense of cost in which wages are an element, the variation of the latter from employment to employment is an irrelevant consideration. Again we find such an observation as the following: " The relative wages of the labour necessary for producing different commodities affect their value just as much as the relative quantities of labour." [1] In the chapter on Ricardo, we saw how this form of expression originated, and determined what the comparatively simple truth is which it so awkwardly conveys. Wages cost, instead of affecting values " as much as " labor cost, does the whole of the affecting; and labor cost affects values only as it affects wages cost. The end of it all is, Mill concludes, with Ricardo (and without improvement upon Ricardo), that a variation of the general rate of wages alters the exchange relations of commodities produced with different combinations of " fixed " and " circulating " capital, independently of the comparative labor costs of the same. What is true of Ricardo's statement is true of this. The proposition regarding the effect of a change of the general rate of wages (or of the rate of profits, for one must always accompany the other in the view of Ricardo and Mill) upon " relative values," may be a true dynamical principle; but the qualification of the original labor-cost theory of value which is contained in this is statical. Exchange values are statically out of proportion to comparative labor costs, without any reference to changes in rates of wages and profits. [2] The reason is that interest is an element in entrepreneur's costs as well as wages. Of the total of wages plus interest, in some cases interest may be 30 per cent., in other cases 60 per cent., or virtually any other per cent. Values being in proportion to the total, cannot be in proportion to either element alone. [2]

[1] Vol. i, p. 567.

[2] Mill emphasizes the fact that he is considering the causes of variations in values. It remains true that both he and Ricardo should have considered the causes of statical aberration of values from the standard of labor cost.

[3] It may be useful to recall the explanation Ricardo made of his posi-

5. Up to the present point, Mill has not taken a decided stand in favor of any qualification of the labor-cost theory which Ricardo had not also approved. In his treatment of skilled labor he admits of a further qualification. Ricardo handled the subject in a very unsatisfactory manner. While he gave the appearance of finding no difficulty for his law of value in skilled labor, he unconsciously evaded the real question at issue. Mill writes:

" When the wages of an employment permanently exceed the average rate, the value of the thing produced will, in the same degree, exceed the standard determined by mere quantity of labour. Things, for example, which are made by skilled labour, exchange for the produce of a much greater quantity of unskilled labour; for no reason but because the labour is more highly paid." [1]

The plain implication of this passage is that skilled labor receives remuneration out of proportion to the quantity of labor rewarded. Therefore it is also implicit that quantity of disutility is what determines quantity of labor. Since labor cost operates upon exchange values only by way of wages cost, in so far as wages cease in fact to be an accurate index of real labor cost, a new difficulty is created for the labor theory—one very important in principle. Mill him-

tion with regard to this point. " I have not said, because one commodity has so much labour bestowed upon it as will cost £1000 and another so much as will cost £2000 that therefore one would be of the value of £1000 and the other of the value of £2000, but I have said that their value will be to each other as two to one. . . . . It is of no importance to the truth of this doctrine, whether one of these commodities sells for £1100 and the other for £2200, or one for £1500 and the other for £3000." (Gonner ed. Ricardo's *Principles*, p. 39.) The interest qualification signifies that the commodities may exchange at other ratios than two to one.

[1] Vol. i, p. 566.

self lays little emphasis upon this point. He regards the superior remuneration of skilled labor as due virtually to a failure of perfect competition. In presenting the subject in this light, he anticipates the important theory of non-competing groups later developed by Cairnes:

" We have before remarked that the difficulty of passing from one class of employments to a class greatly superior, has hitherto caused the wages of all those classes of labourers, who are separated from one another by any very marked barrier, to depend more than might be supposed upon the increase of the population of each class, considered separately; and that the inequalities in the remuneration of labour are much greater than could exist if the competition of the labouring people generally could be brought practically to bear on each particular employment." [1]

It is hardly necessary or advisable to define perfection of competition in such broad terms as to make it require that the remuneration of skilled labor should be reduced to the standard of disutility of labor. In any event, the tendency of remuneration to approach such a level is ineffective, and therefore negligible. Static principles may be conditioned upon assumptions contrary to fact, but the assumptions are never to be made so violent that the law is not an effective force which must be apprehended before dynamic reality can be explained. Under perfect competition, properly defined, skilled labor is still a thorn in the flesh of the old theory of value.

6. It remains to summarize Mill's view of the relation of labor cost to exchange value, and to compare it with the views of Ricardo, Malthus and Senior. In Mill's own language we find the following summary: If one thing ex-

[1] Vol. i, pp. 566-7.

changes for more than another, the cause must be that "it requires for its production either a greater quantity of labor," or (1) "a kind of labour permanently paid at a higher rate," or (2) "the capital which supports that labour must be advanced for a longer period," or, lastly, (3) "the production is attended with some circumstance which requires to be compensated by a permanently higher rate of profit." "Of these elements, the quantity of labor required for the production is the most important; the effect of the others is smaller, though none of them is insignificant." [1]

The qualification which we have numbered one (1) is an addition to Ricardo's list of qualifications. Number two (2) is Ricardo's own work; and of number three (3) he is aware, though he abstracts from it with his customary facility. [2] In the end, we may say that Mill placed more stress on qualifications of the labor theory than did Ricardo. Senior made both ground rent and the superior wages of skilled labor causes of qualification of the labor-cost theory. Mill took Senior's view of skilled labor, but took his stand with Ricardo on the general question of ground rent.

[1] Vol. i, p. 590.

[2] See Ricardo, *Principles*, p. 83. "Let us suppose that all commodities are at their natural price, and consequently that the profits of capital in all employments are exactly at the same rate, or differ only so much as, in the estimation of the parties, is equivalent to any real or fancied advantage which they possess or forego."

CHAPTER X

CAIRNES

1. THE political economy of J. E. Cairnes is virtually a treatise on value and distribution.[1] The points in his work which are of interest to our present purpose are his analysis of cost of production and his famous innovation, the theory of non-competing groups.[2] The views of Cairnes resemble those of Senior in many ways, and are exceedingly destructive of the labor-cost theory, more so than he seemed to realize or cared to admit.

The conditions essential to the existence of value are given as utility, difficulty of attainment, and transferableness.[3] This is Senior's statement with the inferior term, " difficulty of attainment " substituted for " limitation in supply." How the substitution could be made in the face of Senior's reasons against it, is one of the ever-recurring riddles in the history of the philosophy that in some way cost is the essence of value. The theory of value is, according to the best usage of the day, initiated by a discussion of supply and demand. Cairnes posed as a critic of Mill's

[1] *Some Leading Principles of Political Economy Newly Expounded.* London, 1874.

[2] A third point might be taken up were it not for the fact that Cairnes's treatment of it is hardly worthy of consideration. This is his rebuttal against the then newly appeared utility theory of Jevons. Cairnes seems to have had virtually no understanding of the point Jevons was trying to make.

[3] P. 9.

conception of the law of supply and demand, but Professor Marshall has shown conclusively that Mill was correct in substance while Cairnes was not.[1] Following Mill, Cairnes next proceeds to cost of production as an influence fundamental to that of supply and demand. " The supply of a commodity tends to adapt itself to the demand at the normal price," or at that price which just suffices to yield to the producers " the average and usual remuneration on such sacrifices as they undergo." [2] These sacrifices are the elements which constitute cost of production. In the formal definition of cost, Cairnes makes it include " the ultimate elements—labour, abstinence, and risk." [3] But the coördinate position of risk is not maintained. For, in the discussion of cost in detail, risk to laborers is held to be a factor in labor cost, and risk to capitalists a factor in abstinence cost.

" We find labour as an element of cost of production measurable by reference to three of its incidents, and to three of its incidents only—1st. the duration of the exertion, or the quantity of labour, 2d. its severity, or irksomeness; and 3d. the risk attending it." [4]

[1] See Marshall's *Principles*, 3rd ed., p. 172, note, and also the reference there cited, *Fortnightly Review*, April, 1876.

[2] P. 41. Cairnes claims, with great justice, that his term "normal value" or "normal price" is superior to the old terms "natural" and "necessary" price (p. 46).

[3] P. 82.

[4] P. 88. It is a waste of terms to call the duration and quantity of labor the same thing, and consequently to consider the quantity of labor cost and quantity of labor different things. Smith and Ricardo merely touched on this matter, but the former says in a passage incorporated also by the latter in his text: "There may be more labour in an hour's hard work than in two hours early business;" or quantity of labor is the product of duration multiplied by disutility per unit of time; and this is the preferable usage.

As for abstinence:

" the sacrifice will be measured by the quantity of wealth abstained from, taken in connection with the risk incurred, and multiplied by the duration of the abstinence." [1]

With this much said, Cairnes drops risk from consideration. We may follow his example in the present chapter, since the precise relation of risk or risk-taking to cost of production need not be decided in order to determine the import of Cairnes's work for the labor theory.

2. In Cairnes we find a repetition of the protest of Senior against the definition of cost from the point of view of the capitalist-entrepreneur. Thus Cairnes is "compelled to dissent" from the "radically unsound" doctrine of Mill, that wages and profits compose cost of production.

" Of all ideas within the range of economic speculation, the two most profoundly opposed to each other are cost and the reward of cost. * * * Cost and remuneration are economic antitheses of each other. * * * Now in the analysis of cost of production which I have quoted [*i. e.* Mill's] these two opposites are identified." [2]

Cost cannot be defined from " the partial and limited standpoint of the capitalist-employer." [3]   Cairnes makes an excellent and eloquent plea for his idea, but truly all that can be conceded to him is that the two kinds of cost must be scrupulously distinguished, and that propositions true only of disutility costs must not be affirmed of entrepreneur's costs, and *vice versa.*. As for the views of Mill, this economist stated that wages and interest are rewards as well

----

[1] P. 97.   Abstinence is described as a " negative " sacrifice except for the "small positive element of risk."

[2] P. 50.   [3] P. 58.

as costs. The gross inconsistencies, however, of Mill's language in different parts of his book justify scathing criticism.

3. Cairnes does not quit the subject of the measurement of the subjective cost without turning his attention to an incidental problem not touched, I believe, by his predecessors. He states that the effort required to produce a given result does not represent the same sacrifice for different persons, being one thing for the strong or experienced and another for the weak or untrained. Similarly a given sum of capital may stand for no appreciable self-denial on the part of the person contributing it, if he be rich, but for very rigid self-denial if he be poor or in moderate circumstances. How are such differences, Cairnes asks, to be dealt with in computing the cost of production?

" The sacrifices to be taken account of, and which govern exchange value, are, not those undergone by A, B, or C, but the average sacrifices undergone by the class of labourers or capitalists to which the producers of the commodity belong." [1]

In view of the fact that the word *average* as often serves to cover up the lack of an explanation as it serves to explain, Cairnes would have done well to be a little more explicit. As the present writer understands it, a few additional words will place his idea beyond possible misconception. If we call the capitalists who can furnish a given sum of capital at a small sacrifice, and the laborers who can furnish a given amount of labor (in the sense of productive power) at a small sacrifice, strong producers, and call others who are situated in reverse circumstances from these, weak producers, Cairnes's proposition about " average sacrifice " means that " within a given field of competition " we may expect the individually strong and individually weak

[1] P. 95.

producers to be thoroughly and uniformly intermingled. With this meaning, the statement certainly commands assent. With this idea understood, we are able to speak of the labor of coal miners as being harder than that of dry-goods salesmen, without thought of the unusual cases where a very healthy miner suffers less fatigue and discomfort than an invalid salesman.

4. Proceeding with labor and abstinence as cost of production, Cairnes describes the relation of cost to value in terms clearer than any before attained in the regular line of English *"Principles."* Wages and " profits " are derived from the value of the product, and " absorb the whole of that value,"

" with the exception of the case where rent is also an element in the value of commodities—a case which, those acquainted with the economic theory of rent will perceive, does not affect the general argument." [1]

These words make the sum total of Cairnes's discussion of rent, though he has written a large volume devoted chiefly to value and distribution. Value is then everywhere divided into wages and profits. If these wages and profits are in proportion to the sacrifices remunerated, value is in proportion to the sum of these sacrifices, or cost of production. The question, then, becomes definite. Are wages everywhere in proportion to the labor for which they are paid, and is interest an amount proportionate to the abstinence remunerated? Strange as it may seem, this simple question—the affirmative answer to which is necessary to establish the regulation of exchange value by " real " or subjective cost of production—was never proposed by Mill or any of his classical predecessors.

[1] Pp. 62–3.

5. To answer this question, it is first necessary to inquire how far effective competition is realized in actual industry (*i. e.*, in English industry, and for purposes of present-day theory, English industry of Cairnes's time is a very proper system to consider) ; for wages and profits will be in proportion to the sacrifices undergone " wherever, and only so far as competition prevails among producers," and laborers and capitalists have an " effective choice " in selecting from the various occupations in the industrial field. First, Cairnes gives a very clear explanation of the process by which the flow of capital and labor can be redistributed over the industrial field without the transfer of individual units already specialized.[1] This disposes of some exaggerated and erroneous ideas regarding the failure of competition; but the next step is taken by Cairnes himself, who points out an important limitation of competition not emphasized by previous writers. This limitation applies only to the competition of laborers :

" The competition of capital being as we have seen, effective over the entire industry of each commercial country, it follows that so much of the value of commodities as goes to remunerate the capitalist's sacrifice * * * will correspond throughout the range of domestic industry with that portion of the cost which falls to the capitalist.[2]

Not so in the case of labor :

" What we find, in effect, is, not a whole population competing indiscriminately for all occupations, but a series of industrial layers, superposed on one another, within each of which the various candidates for employment possess a real and effective power of selection, while those occupying the several strata are, for all purposes of effective competition,

[1] Pp. 65–70. [2] P. 74.

practically isolated from each other." * * * "We are thus compelled to recognize the existence of non-competing industrial groups as a feature of our social economy." [1]

6. It follows from this that the exchange relations of commodities produced by laborers in different industrial groups are "not governed by the principle of cost of production." And the result is much complicated, because even a single commodity is "very frequently" the product of the labor of more than one industrial group.[2] The terms of exchange between two commodities will be "governed by more than one principle."

"So far as the two commodities are the products of workmen in competition with each other, their values will be governed by cost of production, but so far as they proceed from workmen not in mutual competition, they will be governed by that other principle, yet to be ascertained, which governs normal values in the absence of competition." [3]

It "generally happens that the bulk of the value of each commodity follows one law, * * * while a small remaining element is governed" by the other law.[4] This unsatisfactory idea is at times better expressed in another way, namely, the law of costs governs a good's value in exchange with commodities produced by the same order of laborers, but not in exchange with commodities produced by different orders.

---

[1] Pp. 72-3. Cairnes makes the same classification of the industrial population into groups that Mill made. For criticism and a new classification see Giddings, "The Persistence of Competition," *Political Science Quarterly*, vol. ii, p. 69 *et seq.*; and J. B. Clark, "The Limits of Competition," *ibid.*, p. 45 *et seq.*

[2] P. 76. "Very frequently" ought really to be "nearly always."

[3] P. 76.   [4] P. 80.

"The true conception of the law of cost is thus, not of a law governing universally the values of any class of commodities, but that of one governing the values of certain commodities in certain exchanges."[1]

7. We come now to the second coördinate principle of value, existing in addition to the principle of cost of production, and held to divide with it the control of actual values. This is the so-called law of reciprocal demand. It is simply Mill's law of reciprocal demand as developed by him to explain international values, applied by Cairnes to the "strictly parallel case" of inter-group values. International and inter-group values, or the relative prices of the products of different nations or of different groups,

"do not vary at random irrespective of rule or measure, but exhibit precisely the same tendency to gravitate towards a central point as is manifested in those exchanges which are governed by cost of production."[2]

These words surely attribute a very exact control of values to the "principle of reciprocal demand." But after perusing a very interesting piece of text (pp. 99-105), in which Cairnes applies Mill's doctrine of international value, point by point, to the problem of non-competing groups, we come upon a very important difference between this principle and that of cost in respect to control of values.

"They each * * furnish a centre about which market values gravitate; but there is this difference between the two cases: The centre furnished by Cost of Production stands related to the fluctuations of the individual commodity; that supplied by Reciprocal Demand to the average fluctuations of considerable aggregates of commodities. A reduction in the

[1] P. 80.   [2] P. 98.

cost of producing a hat will lower its price. * * But an alteration in the reciprocal demand of two trading nations (or of two non-competing groups) will act upon the price not of any commodity in particular but of every commodity which enters into the trade. What such an alteration necessitates is a change in the *average* terms on which the trade is carried on; but *it decides nothing as to the details by which the required average shall be attained and maintained.* * * * In the interchanges of non-competing domestic groups, what the reciprocal demand of the groups determines is the average relative level of prices within each group; the distribution of price among the individual products being regulated by the cause which governs value within it, namely, cost of production." [1]

It develops that the law of reciprocal demand fails completely of being a principle coördinate with, and similar to, that of costs. Instead of ruling exchange values in the same way as cost of production, only in another field, it turns out that the force of reciprocal demand is incapable of determining the value of any single good. The principle of reciprocal demand fails signally of fulfilling Cairnes's promise of a principle other than that of cost, which will provide for a central point of gravitation of inter-group exchange ratios. The purport of the argument of Cairnes is no more than this: the law of reciprocal demand merely requires the general level of international exchange values to be such that in the long run the exports of a nation just discharge its liabilities, or, in other words, that its exports and imports will be led to balance, except for the payment of interest on foreign debts, cost of carriage to foreign ship-owners, *etc.* Cairnes applies the law without changing line or point to interchange between non-competing groups.

[1] Pp. 105–6. The italics are mine except for the word "average."

8. It is not necessary, in view of our present purpose, to enter further into the nature of the law of reciprocal demand. The question of importance to us is the effect on the labor-cost theory of value of the doctrine of non-competing groups. Cairnes's famous doctrine merely adds emphasis to a point already made by Senior, namely, that the wages of skilled labor are out of proportion to the amount of labor cost remunerated. Though Cairnes rejects the definition of cost as entrepreneur's cost, his whole argument signifies that subjective cost, or pain cost, can control market value only by way of controlling the wages and interest elements which compose entrepreneur's cost. As for the element of interest, Cairnes, like Senior, holding interest to be paid for abstinence, places it upon an independent basis of subjective cost, and makes it logically coördinate with wages; and Cairnes would treat the difficulty of interest, or the difficulty of " the different proportions of fixed and circulating capital," not as Ricardo did, but precisely as Senior did.[1] As for the element of wages cost, the doctrine of non-competing groups signifies that the comparative wages cost of different commodities may fail to represent their comparative labor costs, or specifically, that they do so fail, when we compare the cost of commodities produced by different non-competing groups. Even if labor cost were the only kind of subjective cost that the entrepreneur has to remunerate, true labor cost would still fail to control exchange values, because the comparative wage expenses of entrepreneurs are not in proportion to the true amount of labor remunerated in each case.

[1] That is to say, for Senior and Cairnes, interest is no longer an unexplained difficulty in the way of the cost philosophy of value, but the conception of cost has been widened so as to include and explain the case of interest. Cairnes has no longer a labor-cost philosophy, but a subjective cost philosophy of value.

In the view of Cairnes, skill as such cannot be called an element in cost of production. But skill may be, and generally is, he continues,

" an indication of that which is an element in cost—namely, the sacrifice whether in the form of labor or abstinence, undergone in acquiring the skill. * * * The point to be attended to is that the addition made to the cost of production [*i. e.* by the employment of skilled labor] is in proportion * * * [only] to the sacrifice." [1]

If competition were effective between groups of laborers, it would result that wages would be forced to correspond with the disutility of labor in all employments, skilled or unskilled (the disutility of acquiring the skill being weighed by the competitors along with the daily disutility of the occupation). In the absence of effective competition—namely, under the actual conditions of non-competing groups—skilled labor generally receives a wage beyond that proportionate to the comparative disutility, past and present, incidental to it.

Cairnes himself refused to regard his innovations as causing any substantial damage to the older theories, for of his whole doctrine of non-competing groups, he says:

" In effect the point in question is of little more than theoretic importance. As a point of theory it is proper to notice it, but the circumstance it deals with has little sensible effect on the facts of exchange." [2]

9. In the opinion of Cairnes, then, there is a failure of the law of costs due to a *failure of competition*. Since Ricardo expressly postulated " perfect competition " as a condition essential to his theory, it might seem as if the

[1] P. 84.   [2] P. 78.

difficulty of non-competing groups is one against which he has taken the necessary precautions. This, however, can hardly be the case. Ricardo's discussion of the subject of skilled labor is so indefinite that his intentions, with respect to the meaning of the words " perfect competition " in this connection, are not obvious. But, in all probability, Ricardo could not have meant that the postulate of perfect competition provides against the wages of skilled labor being in excess of those of common labor. For if he had meant this, he would not have written the section he gives us on skilled labor.[1] In this he says, in effect, that the degree in which different kinds of skilled labor enjoy higher wages does not change greatly from time to time (this itself an error), and that nothing more need be said, since he is considering only the causes of *change of " relative "* *values* (this is also incorrect).

We will take it for granted, then, that by his assumption of free competition Ricardo did not intend to abstract from the difficulty of skilled labor. We certainly could not approve of such a procedure if he had adopted it; for there is so little tendency for actual competition to remove the superior remuneration of skill, that this tendency should not be recognized among legitimate or effective static forces.[2]

[1] *Principles*, chapter i, section iii. *Cf.* chap. v, sec. iv of the present essay.

[2] The validity of a theory is not proved if *some* tendency can be shown to be in keeping with it. The tendency must be *effective*. When the forces that oppose a tendency are relatively great, or the mere obstacles in its way relatively immovable, the tendency cannot be assigned the rank of a force or be laid down as an economic law, not even a static law. True, the difference between an effective and an inoperative tendency is only one of degree. This makes it difficult to decide upon the claims of a proposed law in the particular case, but this is a difficulty which cannot be avoided. The weaker the tendencies taken cognizance

The conclusion is that Ricardo did not examine the problem of skilled labor sufficiently, and that the work of Senior, and especially of Cairnes, shows that in this problem there resides a grave difficulty for the labor theory.   Neither Senior nor Cairnes took occasion specifically to point this out themselves.   To discover that such is the effect of their writings becomes the task of the historian of theory. Though Cairnes refuses to give the name " cost " to entrepreneur's expenses, at bottom his teaching means that the labor cost " philosophy " of value cannot be true, because it is in conflict with the more certain " empirical " laws of value.

of in a given static theory, the more idealistic or refined is that theory. And, at least after a certain point is reached, the more refined the theory becomes, in this sense, the less its degree of validity.   To illustrate this, we need but to refer to the present question of skilled labor.   Throughout the classical economics runs the idea that the superior remuneration of skill really rewards the extra disutility necessarily undergone in acquiring the skill.   Now, if the movement of men among occupations were calculated solely with reference to this disutility, and were free enough, the actual wage of skilled labor could be said to be adjusted to the disutility of the occupation, including the past disutility of acquiring the skill.   The extra part of the wage would be a sort of interest on disutility already expended, as suggested expressly by Adam Smith and by Senior.   But we need not pursue this idea into its minor complications. The point desired to be made is that the tendency for actual wages of skilled labor to adjust themselves to the disutility of the skilled labor is so submerged (permit a questionable metaphor) beneath other forces, that it makes a theory over-refined to recognize it as a law.   I believe it possible to justify nearly all the older theories of value by making a static state to order for each writer, that is, by making one over-refined enough.   Put in other words, so far as the older economists were not guilty of self-inconsistencies, their theories could be justified by granting them sufficient *assumptions*.   The latter is what we refuse to do. An example of a legitimate static law is that wages tend to equal the specific value-product of labor, as contrasted with the theory that wages tend to adjust themselves to the disutility *of the task* performed.

CHAPTER XI

THE ULTIMATE RELATION OF COST TO VALUE

1. The history contained in the preceding ten chapters covers but a limited number of English writers. At the time of writing, a short list of economists was drawn up in advance, which enumerated the thinkers at that time generally regarded as the leaders in the development of the old English political economy. It was stated at the outset that the purpose was to review the opinions of these writers only. An endeavor was made to define this purpose as being to make an *intensive* rather than an *extensive* study of the history of English theory. By an extensive study we should mean the effort to discover writers who have made important contributions to the thought the history of which is being traced, but have been previously unrecognized or insufficiently accredited. Such examinations into the history of English economic literature will probably in the immediate future result in important alterations in what might be called our accepted lists of chief writers. It will be found that thinkers now supposed to have expressed the doctrines of their time with the greatest clearness and power were in some cases surpassed in these points by writers at present almost or quite forgotten. Or it will be found perhaps that new ideas—such for instance as the conception of marginal utility—really originated earlier than at present supposed.

A brief time elapsed between the writing of the tenth and the eleventh chapters of this essay. But in this period there has been published a discussion of the work of some earlier British economists, which establishes beyond a doubt that the marginal utility theory of value was conceived and formulated in most excellent fashion by an English writer as early as 1833, two decades before Gossen and a generation before Menger, Jevons and Walras. The English writer was W. F. Lloyd, Professor of Political Economy at Oxford. A full description of Lloyd's theory, with citations showing the excellence of its statement, appeared in *The Economic Journal*, over the signature of Professor Seligman, of Columbia University.[1] Professor Seligman has called attention to still another writer of great consequence because of his contributions to the theory of value. This is Mountifort Longfield who, as Professor Seligman states, in 1833 gave an able exposition of what is now the modern doctrine of marginal demand and marginal cost.[2]

Avoiding the larger task involved in the extensive study of the history of the theory of value in England, the present monograph has endeavored to interpret the labor theory as it passed through the minds of some nine economists beginning with Smith and ending with Cairnes. The history is that of a subjective-cost philosophy of value and the difficulties of its application to explain the facts of industry. According to this philosophy, or this ultimate explanation, utility is a condition essential to the existence of value, but cost or difficulty of attainment is the *essence* of value. The idea was elucidated by a variety of figures of speech. Utility was conceived as a sort of resting-ground for value, but the height of value

---

[1] "On Some Neglected British Economists," *Economic Journal*, v. xiii, pp. 357–363.

[2] *Ibid.*, p. 527.

upon this ground, the value as an *amount*, was held to be determined by or measured by cost of production. Thus Ricardo wrote to J. B. Say:

The utility of things is incontestably the *foundation* of their value, but the degree of their utility cannot be the measure of their value. . . . The difficulty of [a thing's] production is the sole measure of its value.[1]

Karl Marx was accustomed to speak of value as "a congelation of human labor," and to speak of a useful object, or an object made useful in the process of production, as a sort of receptacle for value.

In his involved "philosophical" account of value, as we termed it, Adam Smith taught that the value, or "real worth," of a good is measured equally well by the amount of labor which it has cost to produce, or by the labor which it can command in exchange. When, however, Adam Smith turns his attention to the proximate principles of value in the actual competitive market, we find him confessing that the theory which he first developed applies without modification only to a primitive state of society, without land rent and interest on capital. In this primitive state the amount of labor which a commodity costs determines the amount of labor which it can command in exchange. Under the conditions of advanced society, the rent of land and the "profits of stock" must come out of the exchange value of the product, and the labor cost of the latter, which is paid for by wages, no longer determines its value.[2] If we take advantage of modern terminology, and throw

[1] See *ante*, pp. 44–5.

[2] Adam Smith nevertheless retains the " labor-command " measure of value as applicable to the conditions of advanced society, for criticism of which see *ante*, pp. 30 and 39.

Adam Smith's theory into our own words, we make its precise significance clearer. It means virtually that the exchange value of a good in the fully developed social economy is determined by its *entrepreneur's* or *money* cost of production, so far as it is determined by cost at all. Competition must be perfect to enable cost to determine actual values. Entrepreneur's cost is composed of expenditures for wages of the labor, rent of the land, and "profits" of the capital necessary for production. The labor cost of producing the commodity determines only the amount of the wages cost to the entrepreneur. The other elements helping to make the total of entrepreneur's cost are not determined by the labor cost of producing the commodity. Thus the exchange value of a good is determined by its entrepreneur's cost, but this latter is not determined by labor cost, and consequently the exchange value of the good is not determined by labor cost. The existence of rent and interest destroys the regulation of exchange values by labor cost. It must be kept in mind that all this is very much more explicit than what Adam Smith said. It signifies that the labor-cost philosophy of value cannot be true—perhaps Smith would say only that it is imperfect or not precisely true—because it is in conflict with a more certain empirical law of value, namely, the law of entrepreneur's cost.

Ricardo adopted the labor-cost philosophy of value virtually as a premise, and the most important parts of his reasoning on the subject are concerned with removing or minimizing the empirical difficulties with this philosophy.[1] In the end he admitted that interest is an

[1] Since the chapter on Ricardo herein contained was written, it has been suggested to the writer that he is mistaken in attributing any

element in that form of cost which exercises the most
direct and compelling influence on exchange values. He
made concessions, which pursued to their logical outcome, signify that the existence of interest throws the
exchange values of goods out of proportion to their pure
labor costs of production. We have seen how he put
this concession in a peculiar and misleading manner.[1]
As for rent of land, Ricardo hastens to repudiate Adam
Smith's admission that it also is a source of difficulty to
the labor theory. He gets rid of rent by explaining that

"philosophical" account whatsoever to Ricardo, that in fact Ricardo's
whole treatment is purely empirical. The writer cannot concur in this
judgment. It is admitted that Ricardo virtually takes this philosophy
for granted, instead of endeavoring to establish it, but the almost appalling confusion into which his exposition of value falls when the difficulty
of interest is reached (see *ante*, chap. v, §§ 5-9) can be explained, so it
is believed, only according to Wieser's interpretation of Ricardo's work.
This is, namely, that he is endeavoring to force the empirical principles,
or the "facts" of entrepreneur's cost, to fit the labor philosophy. A
thinker who confined himself to a purely empirical analysis would never
reach the labor-cost thesis with which Ricardo opens at once his chapter
on value and his *Principles of Political Economy*. The thesis is *a
priori*, that is, as contrasted with the theory of entrepreneur's cost. If
Ricardo were working with merely an empirical account of value, and
were not embarrassed by an uncertain philosophy of value, how would
he ever come to speak of the cost of production, which determines value,
as consisting of "labor and profits!" He should say "wages and
profits." Again, how would he be led to commence his chapter on
"Natural and Market Price," by the assertion that the market price of
a commodity can deviate temporarily from its "natural price, or the
quantity of labor which it has cost!" No empirical theory would lead
to the statement that the normal price toward which competition forces
actual prices is a *quantity of labor*. This natural price is Adam Smith's
"philosophical" natural price or "first price," namely, labor.

[1] He stated it in the form of an admission that, besides changes in
labor cost, there can be a second cause of *variations* of the exchange
ratios between commodities, namely a rise or fall of the general rate of
interest. He first stated the second cause to be a fall or rise of the
general rate of wages, but in his view this is equivalent to a rise or fall
of "profits," *i. e.*, interest. See *ante*, chap. v, §§ 7 and 8.

the exchange values of commodities are regulated by the
quantity of labor required for production on the least
fertile land in use, or the quantity required to produce
the most expensive portions of the supplies.   In modern
phraseology, he urged that it is not the actual labor cost
of a good but its marginal labor cost, which regulates
its value.   Ricardo himself used that fatally ambiguous
formula, "rent does not enter into price."   Having removed rent by making the value determining cost marginal, and having minimized the difficulty of interest,
Ricardo proceeded as if the labor theory were, for the
sake of argument, intact.

The chief purport of the work of Malthus was, first,
to deny Ricardo's right to disregard the interest difficulty and, second, to reaffirm Adam Smith's opinion that
land rent also throws values out of relation to labor
costs.   Turning now to Senior, who was the next writer
to suggest a worthy and new idea, we find that in the
view of this economist the existence of land rent and interest as elements in entrepreneur's cost is fatal to the
labor theory.   But Senior explained interest as the reward for abstinence, just as wages are the reward for
labor.   In his view labor and abstinence are independent,
co-ordinate elements in subjective cost.[1]   However, the
more important idea that can be extracted from Senior's
reasonings is that wages as actually paid are not in proportion to the quantities of labor engaged in different
employments.   For in his view all skilled labor gains a
wage which really includes a rent to "scarce natural
talents."[2]

[1] Senior—the attacks of Marx upon him notwithstanding—was far
from assigning to these two elements equal ethical importance.

[2] Senior's rent to skill is an entirely different form of surplus from
that due to the excess of utility produced above disutility incurred in the

Summing up the results of Senior's argument for ourselves (since he himself did not make the present applications of his doctrines), the labor theory requires that the entrepreneur's costs of commodities should be in proportion to their labor costs, but entrepreneur's costs are out of proportion to labor costs, not only because they include rent of land and interest on capital, but because the very payments of wages themselves may be out of proportion to the comparative amounts of labor employed and remunerated. When we say that entrepreneur's costs are out of proportion to labor costs, we do not mean that they are in excess of wages cost, though they are this, but that for commodity A to cost the same quantity of labor as commodity B, is not a sign that the two commodities have the same entrepreneur's costs. In other words, relative entrepreneur's costs are not determined by relative labor costs.

John Stuart Mill took Ricardo's view of land rent and of interest, but took Senior's view that skilled labor occasions the entrepreneur an expense out of proportion to the *quantity of labor* remunerated. That is to say, he

"earlier" parts of the working day of all labor. So long as the length of the working day is left to the worker himself, he will stop when the terminal utility and disutility are equivalent. All previous parts of the day produce a surplus of utility. This is the surplus which occupies an important place in J. B. Clark's theory of value. Compare Marshall's "producer's" and "consumer's rents." Senior's "rent to scarce natural talents" is explicable only on the supposition that the disutility endured and the return of utility enjoyed by a skilled laborer can be compared with the same quantities for an unskilled laborer. Senior means merely that skilled laborers obtain higher returns at lower sacrifices as compared with unskilled. A certain part of the return enjoyed by the skilled laborer is equivalent to that enjoyed by the common worker; the part in excess of this is the rent. Senior considers it analogous to the rent which goes to lands of superior fertility. Further consideration will be given in a later section to the relation of skill to the labor theory of value.

held that the higher wages of skill do not represent a higher labor cost. This opinion he adopted without at the same time taking up Senior's particular use of the term, "rent to talents." As we concluded at the end of Chapter IX, it may be said that Mill followed Ricardo more closely than any other of his predecessors on the question of the relation of labor to value. Turning to Cairnes we note that this writer gave one sentence in his book to the doctrine of land rent, and in this he acquiesced in the judgment of Ricardo and J. S. Mill. But Cairnes adopted a position with reference to interest identical with that assumed by Senior, and his theory of "non-competing groups" merely emphasizes the claim that the amount of wages paid in different employments is not a test of the quantities of labor employed.

Taking the whole period covered in this history, we see that a goodly number of points of criticism were raised against the pure labor-cost theory. The reader may have noted that all these points were implicit in the work of Senior, and in his alone. Does the entrepreneur's payment of land rent, of interest on capital, and his payment of a superior wage to skilled labor (a wage out of proportion to the disutility of skilled labor), make impossible the theory that labor cost regulates value? Is it not possible that labor cost may be conceived in some way, perhaps as "marginal cost," or "social marginal disutility," such that the exchange values of the products of industry can be shown to depend upon the labor cost of these products? In the following pages the writer will try to give an answer to this question, so far as it lies in his power. It will be indispensable to bear with a considerable number of preliminaries. The ultimate relation of cost (in any or all of its forms) to value, cannot be discussed with any success, unless the

parties to the discussion have reached some understanding as to the relation of utility to value and as to the
meaning of other proposed laws of value than cost laws.
Merely a moderate acquaintance with the contemporary
literature of economic theory gives complete assurance
that the necessary understanding just mentioned cannot
be presumed to exist, but must be established as care-
fully as possible.

2. Historically, there have been two distinct conceptions of cost—at least in English political economy—
namely, (1) labor cost, and (2) entrepreneur's cost.
Logically, there are two elementary forms of cost, (1)
pain cost, and (2) potentiality cost. The first consists
in the human discomforts or undesirable feelings incidental to the production of wealth, whether the disutility
of labor, or that of "abstinence" or "waiting." This is
also frequently called "true," "real," or "subjective"
cost. The terms "true" and "real" are hardly com-
mendable, for the other elementary form of cost is quite
as real as this. The word "subjective" is genuinely distinctive, but probably less so than the generic term
"pain."

The second elementary form of cost is that emphasized
chiefly by the Austrian writers. In the making or
acquisition of economic products, certain scarce agents
are either destroyed, or else for the time being employed
in a way that excludes their employment in the production of other goods. We may say that the production
of any given good involves the destruction of certain
productive agents, or, permitting a convenient liberty of
expression, of the uses of agents from which other goods
might have been produced. Thus with the emergence
of one good the possibility of some other good is excluded. Professors von Wieser and Böhm-Bawerk, who

have written the best explanations of the relation of this form of cost to value, have suggested no distinctive name for it. The reason appears to be that they consider this as the only form of cost which requires especial explanation, since, as they hold, it is the only kind of cost which can be correlated with value. In an article in the *Quarterly Journal of Economics*,[1] Professor D. S. Green has suggested the term "opportunity cost" for the Austrian conception. Professor H. J. Davenport, having in mind the same conception, refers to it as "sacrifice cost."[2] Professor Heinrich Dietzel speaks of the same cost as "*Nutzeneinbusse.*"[3] This concept has also in various places been designated "social cost." Though this cost is social in a certain comparatively irrelevant sense in which the other kind of cost is not social, the term "social cost" is not a good one because it lacks distinctiveness. There is nothing intrinsically social about potentiality cost, nor would the other elementary form of cost, that is, pain cost, be best designated "individual cost." Both forms would appear in an isolated individual economy, for instance in our fictitious but highly useful Crusoe economy. "Sacrifice cost" is ambiguous, because the word "sacrifice" is used as often as not, though perhaps improperly, to signify the discomfort or pain endured in production. A term is needed to distinguish a form of cost from pain cost. "Potentiality" cost appeals to the writer as being a term somewhat better than "opportunity" cost. When certain common production goods, capable of being turned to the making of more than one kind of thing,

[1] January, 1894, p. 218.
[2] In the *Journal of Political Economy*, vol. ii, p. 561.
[3] *Theoretische Socialökonomik*, 1895, vol. i, p. 205.

are used up to make a given thing, their potentiality to make an alternative thing is destroyed. The potentiality cost of a commodity is measured by the highest other value that might have been obtained if this commodity had not been produced from the productive agents entering into it.

If it be correct that pain cost and potentiality cost are the two elementary kinds of cost, what is the relation of the two historical forms of cost, labor and entrepreneur's cost, to these? Just as the word labor stands for two distinct things, toil and productive power, so may "labor cost" mean either pain cost or potentiality cost. If the term labor cost is used without a qualifying adjective or explanatory phrase, it would naturally call up in most minds the conception of pain cost. But labor force is the most disposable of all productive agencies, and when the productive power of labor (what the entrepreneur buys) is used up in the production of a given commodity, we have a perfect example of potentiality cost. As we have seen, Adam Smith used labor at different times, both in the sense of toil or disutility and in the sense of productive power or potential commodity. Ricardo, to the best of the writer's knowledge, said nothing to indicate definitively which of these concepts he designated by the term labor. In the writer's judgment the presumption is that by the labor cost which regulates the exchange value of commodities, Ricardo meant what we call pain cost. At one place, Ricardo said "difficulty of attainment" is the true measure of value. It seems almost assured that this must mean " pain cost." When cost is conceived as the ultimate essence of value, the cost will almost certainly be pain cost or "real cost." It is interesting to note that Professor Dietzel, in arguing that the Ricardian labor theory of value is perfectly reconcilable with all that holds good in the utility theory, states that labor cost must be conceived solely as "*Nutzeneinbusse,*" *i. e.*, utility-sacrifice, or potentiality cost. When the labor theory is founded upon the conception of labor as toil ("Unlust"), he considers it to be "built upon sand." [1]

We see that it is possible to mean either pain or potentiality cost by the words "labor cost." Labor as "pain" and labor as productive power are not the same thing but the first is incident to the second. It remains to consider the relation of entrepreneur's expense to the two elementary forms of cost. Torrens desired to exclude the money outlays of the entrepreneur in interest charges from the money cost of production of a good. That is, he maintained that what he called "profits," the chief constituent of which was interest, is no part of cost of production. This view was never adopted by any subsequent economist of weight. The very simple reasons why it is indefensible were mentioned in the chapter on Torrens. Conceding then that interest is a part of entrepreneur's cost, the relation of the latter to "pain cost" can be stated in a few words. The total "pain cost" of any article, which is produced by entrepreneurs, finds its remuneration in those payments which go to make up *cost* from the viewpoint of the entrepreneur. The point to be held fast, a point already emphasized, is that the subjective costs of goods so produced can influence their exchange values only by way of influencing their entrepreneur's costs.

The relation of entrepreneur's expense to potentiality

---

[1] *Theoretische Socialokonomik*, 1895, vol. 1, p. 233. Dietzel supposes that Smith conceived of labor solely as "*Unlust,*" but in this he is clearly mistaken. See *ante*, chapter iv.

cost is less simple and familiar than the foregoing. It will best be taken up in a subsequent section after we have endeavored to state the gist of the utility theory of value. We may conclude the present discussion of cost concepts by noting that there are several ways of reckoning or analyzing entrepreneur's cost. (1) Adam Smith's method, adopted by Malthus, is set forth in the following definite words written by the latter: "The cost of producing any commodity is made up of all the wages, all the profits, and all the rent which * * * * are necessary to bring that particular commodity to market in the quantity required."[1] (2) Perhaps the most approved modern method of analyzing the elements in entrepreneur's cost is merely into wages and interest. In this case rent paid for the use of land is treated in the same way as rent paid for buildings or for machinery or power. (3) The most direct treatment of entrepreneur's cost defines it shortly as including the prices of all the productive agencies used up in the making of the product, or as the value of raw material, machinery, and labor power "entering into" the product. It is always necessary to explain immediately that some production goods are in no sense consumed in the making of the product. Such are the land and buildings. Some production goods are consumed only in very small part in the making of a single product. The total money cost of a product is according to one system divided into "prime cost" and "establishment cost." The former includes the prices of all those elements which are entirely used up in making the product. The latter includes the product's due share of the money cost of the rest of the establishment, worn to a certain extent or

[1] See *ante*, p. 86.

occupied for a time in its making. Numerous practical formulæ are in use to aid in the difficult problem of imputing to the product its due share in the various general charges. A second necessary explanation connected with the third form of calculating entrepreneur's cost is that, since the prices of the production goods have to be paid before the product is finished, each price must be increased by interest for the time of its advance, to give the complete cost of the product. In order to state the relation of entrepreneur's expense to potentiality cost, it is not necessary to discuss in full the mutual relations of the various modes of calculating entrepreneur's cost. Such a discussion would, it seems to the writer, involve us in the theory of interest and indeed in the entire theory of distribution. Fortunately it is sufficient for our present ends to point out that all forms of analyzing entrepreneur's cost must be based upon the third, or, as we might call it, the practical method. If it is desired to reduce the cost of a product to wages and interest, the practical cost of the article as defined above will have to be ascertained as a starting-point. We will be content in a later section to trace the connection between potentiality cost and the practical form of entrepreneur's cost.

3. It is impossible to give the term *value* any one meaning. The word is so ambiguous that Jevons advocated its abandonment. The central thought of the value concept seems to be *capacity to excite desire*, but there are two grand kinds of economic value which are best designated, (1) exchange value and (2) esteem value.[1]

[1] For an excellent discussion of the term " esteem value " see Walsh, *The Measurement of General Exchange Value*, pp. 1–6. The writer is greatly indebted to Walsh's discussion of the value concept. The two kinds of value here distinguished are the same as those designated objective exchange value and subjective value by the Austrian writers.

The exchange value of an article has often been defined
as a ratio—or specifically, as the ratio in which the unit
of measure of the article exchanges for a multiple, or
fraction, of the unit of measure of any other determinate
thing [1]—and again as the quantity of that other thing for
which it exchanges. But both of these conceptions are
involved in metaphysical difficulties which make them
impossible to employ in actual reasoning, and all writers
are accustomed to make assertions about exchange value
which are not in the least true of these, their purely
formal, definitions. Walsh has shown most clearly that
the only conception of exchange value free from difficulty
is that of *power* in exchange. Exchange value is the
power in a thing by means of which its owner is enabled
to command other things possessing a similar power.[2]
This power is measured objectively by the physical quantity of some other thing selected for the purpose, but the
value is not that quantity, though speaking elliptically we
may say the value of a coat is twenty bushels of wheat or
twenty dollars. The exchanging power in our daily
thought is always and properly referred to the thing and
not to the man or owner. When the thing is gone the
power is gone. The purchasing power of a twenty-
dollar piece does not reside in the holder.[3] It goes with-

[1] As, for instance, by Pantaleoni, *Pure Economics*, p. 123.

[2] This definition by itself does not of course make clear the ultimate
source of this power. For proximate and practical purposes the weight
of a pound nugget of gold might well be defined as its power to counterbalance in the scales a certain piece of metal, the standard troy pound.
This definition contains no hint of the common source of the counterbalancing power of both weights. In the same way the above-given
definition of exchange value ignores a certain common source of all exchange values.

[3] For a discussion of certain avoidable objections that have been made
to the concept of purchasing power, see Walsh, *op. cit.*, pp. 7 and 8.

out saying that this power can exist in an article only
when there is another thing for which it can be exchanged and when there are men to effect the exchanging. It is not implied that articles of commerce have
the power to exchange themselves in market places without human intervention. But the purchasing power resides in the article; it is always referred to the article in
our thought, and it leads to nonsensical results to run
counter to our commonest and most practical forms of
thought and endeavor to locate it elsewhere.

The end of the theory of value is to explain the causes
which govern exchange values, or practically, market
prices. Other conceptions of value than exchange value
derive their just importance in political economy only
from the aid they may render in this explanation. This
defines the place of the conception of esteem value. A
finished explanation of exchange values is impossible
without a theory of esteem values, just as an ultimate
explanation of the counterbalancing powers of different
objects in the scales is vain without the general law of
gravitation. The power of an apple to counterbalance
two eggs might have been thought of as a matter purely
relative between apples and eggs, before the general conception was framed of the common attraction exerted by
the earth upon both apples and eggs. Exchange values
were once stated to be "purely relative." The objectionable point in the statement lies in the adverb "purely."
For exchange values are derived from esteem values very
much as weights, or powers to counterbalance, are derived from the earth's attraction. That is, these two
derivations are generally similar. Here as elsewhere
analogies can be pressed too far. The derivation of the
exchange values of different goods in the social market
from the esteem values put upon these goods by the

consumers, or purchasers in the society, is a process in-
definitely more difficult to explain than the relative
weights of ponderables.[1]   Given the gravity of separate
objects it is but a step to explain their relative weights,
but given the esteem values of different economic commodities it is a long road to follow the process through
which these determine the exchange values of the same
commodities.   If esteem value be the gravity behind exchange value, the case is rendered complex in that each
good possesses a separate esteem value for every different consumer whereas there is but one earth to attract
each object whose relative weight we desire to explain.

In the judgment of the writer, the best definition of
esteem value is " the significance (*Bedeutung*) which concrete goods attain in our estimation when we realize that
we are *dependent* upon them for the satisfaction of some
want."   This is a loose translation of the definition
formulated by Carl Menger in 1871.[2]   The individual
good attains value not simply when it is capable of af-
fording us satisfaction, but when it *conditions* the satisfaction.   Goods existing in superfluity give satisfactions
but do not *condition* them, hence any unit of such goods
possesses no value.   The removal or destruction of a
unit occasions the loss of no satisfaction.   Menger's

---

[1] It takes little discernment to see that this statement is not equivalent
to saying that the formulation of a theory of value is a greater accom-
plishment than was the formulation of the law of gravitation. The
writer does not plead guilty to implying that.

[2] See *Grundsätze der Volkswirthschaftslehre*, Wien, 1871, p. 78.
" Der Werth ist die Bedeutung, welche concrete Güter oder Güterquan-
titäten für uns dadurch erlangen, dass wir in der Befriedigung unserer
Bedürfnisse von der Verfügung über dieselben abhängig zu sein uns
bewusst sind."   Menger gives this as a definition of value simply, but
it is of course a definition of that particular kind of value which we have
agreed to call "esteem value."

definition was a triumph of theory in stating the relation of value to human satisfaction and to utility.

The law of marginal utility is but a corollary of the principle involved in this definition. The utility of a good is its power to afford satisfaction.[1] When goods occur in stocks of like units the phenomenon of "marginal" utility emerges. As the stock of such goods to be used by a consumer within a given time is increased, the satisfaction afforded by each successive unit declines.[2] The actual utility of each successive increment is lower than the actual utility of the preceding increment. The actual utility of the last or marginal increment is the "marginal" utility of any of the increments. The reason why the value of any such increment is determined at the height of its "marginal" utility is only because any one increment conditions merely the satisfaction afforded by the last or marginal increment. Remove or destroy any increment and rationally only the satisfaction of the marginal increment will be given up. In effect any increment is the marginal one. Thus the law of marginal utility is not the fundamental law of value.

[1] Of course this power in the good exists only in relation to some human being. It is perfectly true that the good would have no such power if there were no man to use it, and that its power may change as the condition of the man using it is changed, and that its power over one man is different from its power over another. For these reasons, utility has often been declared to be subjective, as if it resided in the mind of the man. Whether it is subjective or objective depends precisely upon what one means by these terms. Practically we may say that our habitual thought correctly refers the utility to the good and conceives it as an attribute belonging to the good in virtue of its common physical properties. The utility of the good does not exist in the mind except in the sense in which all things exist in the mind. We should at least say that utility has objective reference. The satisfaction belongs to the mind, the utility to the good. The utility is a sort of objective counterpart or projection of the satisfaction.

[2] "Gossen's law."

Menger's definition contains this fundamental law and gives a universal principle of value. The theorem that value depends upon marginal utility is merely a deduction from this fundamental principle, and is of limited scope, since it applies only where there are goods in stocks.[1]

An absolutely essential point to be kept in mind is that the value of an object is not derived from the sacrifice made to obtain it. On the contrary we make the sacrifice because the object has this value. The value is first, the sacrifice second. The only means of estimating how much sacrifice or discomfort we can afford to undergo to obtain an object is by judging its value to us *previously* to and *independently* of the sacrifice. If the labor cost, say, determined the value, we could expend labor cost regardlessly in producing any objects whatsoever. But this is just what we cannot do. We must have a care when we expend labor. A care for what? For the value of the result. The value of the object is derived from the satisfaction which it can afford, but it is attributed to the object only when it is the indispensable condition of that satisfaction.

When a particular object conditions some satisfaction of ours, it possesses a superior power over our welfare to that possessed by a good which, while it affords us satisfaction, does not condition it. It would be a waste of energy to spend it in producing or conserving the thing of inferior power. The ultimate reason why our

---

[1] That is, it applies only where goods are held in stocks by individual consumers. Thus the "esteem" value of a piano commonly has nothing to do with "marginal" utility. Only if consumers were to own pianos in stocks—to use several at once—would there be grounds for speaking of the marginal utility of a piano. For further consideration of this point see the next section.

minds instinctively assign a superior importance to the things of higher power over our welfare is that such instincts contribute to our fitness in the struggle for existence. The things of lower rank possess merely utility. The things of higher rank possess a superior power which we recognize and distinguish as *value*. Lack of this distinction would lead to a waste of energy in the modifications which we effect in our environment.[1]

4. Let us consider now the essential features of the utility theory of value. According to this doctrine the sole source of value is human satisfaction. The thought is well conveyed, though the expression may be somewhat loose, by saying that the only inherently valuable thing is satisfaction, and that the value of satisfaction is passed out to, or attributed to, any external object upon which the satisfaction is dependent. Human satisfactions are quantities, for they are capable of being *more* or *less*. But they are inexact and wavering quantities. Similarly, the esteem values of goods, derived from the satisfactions conditioned by these goods, are quantitative, but are incapable of exact or constant numerical expression. The exchange values of goods are exact and relatively constant quantities. Nevertheless, exchange values are assuredly founded upon esteem values. The description of the process by which these wavering and more or less uncertain esteem values determine the exact and definite exchange values of goods, is perhaps the most difficult part of the utility theory. But

[1] Professor v. Wieser explains that the reason why we attribute a superior importance to a good that has marginal utility as compared with a good that is superabundant, is because we have a "natural indifference" toward goods in general, which can only be overcome when the good is so scarce that its absence would decrease our satisfactions. *Natural Value*, p. 29. This would seem to be explaining the thing by itself. The ultimate origin of this "natural indifference" is what calls for explanation.

without this part—commonly called the "theory of price"—the utility doctrine remains a mere torso.

Böhm-Bawerk's theory of price is the only attempt that has been made to complete the utility theory in this direction, which is at once well known and authoritative.[1] Though the fundamental lines of this explanation are correct, it is in externals at least defective in two noteworthy respects. In the first place, one of its principal assumptions is untrue to the typical conditions of exchange under the division of labor. This assumption consists in supposing that sellers' subjective valuations are effective factors in determining price in the market of an organic society. In Böhm-Bawerk's theory, the reader will recall, the miniature but supposedly typical market is assumed to consist of a number of sellers owning horses and a number of buyers desiring them. The first step in the argument is to assign a money expression to the esteem or "subjective" value of a horse to each buyer and each seller. Then if these money expressions, or "price equivalents," are higher for some one buyer than for some one seller an exchange of money for a horse is possible between the two. If buyer B values a horse at $45 and seller S at $40, B can afford to part with, and S can afford to take for a horse any sum of money over $40 and under $45. By considering all the price equivalents of sellers on one side and of buyers on the other side, Böhm-Bawerk shows us that for every given combination of such figures in a market there is a certain definite number of sales possible, and these sales must take place at a price fixed between the price equivalents of the last buyer and the last seller. In other words, the market price will be fixed between the money valuations set upon a horse by the "marginal pair."

[1] *Positive Theory of Capital,* book iv, especially chap. iv.

The region so delimited by the marginal pairs becomes narrower as the number of buyers and sellers entering the market increases.   Thus, in a large market the price is virtually determined to a point.   The difficulty with this theory is that under the division of labor, sellers make products for the market, in view of the market price, and make them in numbers and keep them in stocks far in excess of their own needs.   Under the division of labor, the lowest price at which a seller will part with a commodity is not set by the marginal utility or subjective value of the commodity to him.   A theory of price applicable to the modern market must not employ the subjective valuations of sellers as a factor in price determination.

In the second place, Böhm-Bawerk's theory of price is misleading, since it obscures the fact that the Austrian theory of value always assumes the supply of the goods whose value it is to explain.   The Austrian writers themselves teach us that the value of a good depends upon the supply of it.   The theory of marginal utility explains very well why an increase of supply lowers value or a decrease raises value.   But if there should be any cause which limits or regulates the supply of goods with reference to their value, *by some kind of an adjustment to value,* this cause would be both a cause and a regulator (or at least a part regulator) of value.   Cost of production in some ultimate form is by many writers supposed to be such a cause.   The human " pain cost " of producing goods is of equal importance in theory with the human pleasure gain had from utilizing the goods.   The value of an addition to the stock of a given sort of goods always furnishes a motive for the increase of the stock.   Any cause which limits the supply at a certain point in the face of this human desire for the increase is a cause of value.   True, it is a cause more remote than utility, but still a cause of value.   Since the

Austrian writers virtually ignore the cause or causes governing supply (and thus governing or helping to govern marginal utility itself), the doctrine of price which they advance ought to rest openly and squarely upon the assumption that the supply of the good is taken for granted. In Böhm-Bawerk's theory of price, the total supply of horses in the miniature market is simply assumed, not accounted for.[1] If horses were more plentiful in this market the sellers' price equivalent would be lowered and the market price would turn out lower. It is a fair criticism that Böhm-Bawerk obscures the important point of the dependence of price upon supply, by assigning sellers and buyers an arbitrary series of money valuations as the very first step in his argument.

The " theory of price," as the Austrians call that part of their theory which traces the connection between consummers' " subjective " values and market exchange values, must begin with a clear recognition that the pure utility theory of value assumes outright the extent of the supplies of all goods. Let us, then, inquire first how the price of a given supply of consumption goods is determined.[2]

---

[1] As Professor Macvane exclaims, the Austrians seem to reason as if the good fairies determined what the supply of commodities shall be. See *The Quarterly Journal of Economics,* vol. v, p. 24. Concerning Professor Macvane's general attacks on the Austrian position, it is only fair to say, however, that he appears in the main issues entirely to miss the point of the utility theory. See also the same journal, vol. vii, p. 255, and the *Annals of the American Academy of Political and Social Science,* vol. iv, p. 348.

[2] This enquiry must constitute the first part of the theory of exchange value, since it is quite beyond dispute that cost in any form can influence exchange value only by influencing supply. Value will rest at the level of cost only when the supply of the good is at just the proper point. When the supply is at any other point, as in the case of monopolies, value no longer rests at the level of costs. But value is still determined by certain other influences. The description of these is the first problem.

If a certain supply of some consumption good is presented for sale in the social market, there is theoretically some one price at which just this amount of goods can be sold. Following Professor Marshall, we may call this the "social demand price." At a higher price, only a less supply could be disposed of. At a lower price more could be sold. The competition of buyers ultimately prevents this lower price being set. The dependence of the social demand price of a given supply of goods upon the esteem value of these goods to the consumers in the social market may be traced as follows:

(1) From *esteem values* to *price equivalents*. The sum of money which a consumer would pay for the addition of an article to his possessions rather than go without that article is called its price equivalent. The price equivalent must not be confused with the price he may pay actually to buy the article, namely, the market price. A piano may have a market price of $600, but have a price equivalent of $1,000 to A. If the market price of pianos were to ascend to $1,000, A would still purchase one. But more than $1,000 he would not pay. When A assigns to a piano a price equivalent of $1,000, this sum of money, of course, has significance merely as the representative of the indefinite variety of other goods which A supposes to be within the command of $1,000. Thus A's ability to think out price equivalents depends upon the already existing exchange value of money, or, in other words, upon prices themselves. If the market prices of carpets, carriages, wines and other things were different from what they are, the amount of other things commanded by $1,000 would be altered, and assuredly A's price equivalent for a piano would change. Thus the price equivalent of one thing can be named only in view of previously existing scales of market prices of other things. A consumer comes to form

a conception of the significance of a unit of money to his welfare.   Into the question of the inner nature of this conception we cannot afford here to push our inquiry.   Without this conception he could not set price equivalents.   It is merely a matter of experience that in fact consumers do set price equivalents.   The sole possible explanation of the fact that when a monopoly raises the price of a consumption good the sales of it decline, is that some buyers have been excluded because the price asked for has passed above their price equivalents.[1]   The worth of money to a consumer depends upon the extent of his money income.   Thus the price equivalent set upon a good by any consumer depends (1) upon the esteem value of that good to him, and (2) upon the extent of his money income.   Given a consumer's money income, his price equivalents for various articles will be determined by, and be in proportion to, the esteem values those articles have for him.

(2) From *price equivalents* to *market-price*.   The price at which a given supply of a certain good can be sold to a body of consumers is a *resultant* from their individual price equivalents for this good.   It is in no sense an average or mean of these price equivalents.[2]   This is best understood by imagining the supply of the good offered in the market to be increased by one unit.   This extra unit must be added to some person's stock.   It will go normally to the person who will pay the most for it, but the price of the unit will have to be lowered sufficiently to bring it down to this person's price equivalent for a unit.   In the

[1] If the good be of a kind held by consumers in stocks, it should go without saying that instead of a buyer being entirely excluded by a rise of price, only the marginal increments of his purchases may be excluded.

[2] Employing Professor Marshall's terminology we would say that the " social demand schedule " is a *resultant* from combining all the " individual demand schedules."

open market, then, the prices of all units will have to be lowered to the level of the price of this unit. This illustrates the way in which the social demand price of a given supply of goods is determined at some individual price equivalent. The price of a given supply is determined at the point of a marginal individual price equivalent.

In the last section it was asserted that unless a good is possessed in a plurality of units, that is, in a *stock,* by the individual consumer, its value will not be determined by *marginal* utility. The Austrian writers have made this perfectly clear, but there are innumerable places in the literature which has sprung up about the Austrian theory, either expounding or criticizing it, where the value of such a good as a piano or a furnace is said to depend on marginal utility. Let us suppose that no person possesses more than one piano. In this case, properly speaking there is nothing marginal about the value-determining utility of a piano. There are, however, two methods in vogue of discovering an alleged marginal utility in such a single unit commodity. The first is to point out that a piano may serve several uses. For instance, it may be used to produce music and also as an ornamental piece of furniture. It is then suggested that one of these uses is greater or less than the other and is marginal. Some suggest by implication or directly that it is the least use to which a piano is put which determines its value to the owner. If it should be suggested in reply that a piano might be used to conceal a discolored place in the wall, which could equally well be done by a two-dollar screen, the probable reply would be that it is only the least use to which the piano can be put *economically* which determines its value. Even so acute a writer as Smart [1] is guilty of this perversion. When it

[1] See his *Introduction to the Theory of Value*, p. 37.

is in the pursuit of such margins, the mind is far adrift from the true logic of the utility theory. When a piano is actually used to cover a piece of wall, this is assuredly an "economic" use of the article. This use does not exclude or hamper any of its other uses. It is true no one would pay $600 for a piano merely to cover a bad piece of wall, but very likely few would pay that sum for any one use of the piano. The truth is, the value of a piano to its user depends upon the sum of its uses to him. The value of the piano measures the total amount of satisfaction *conditioned* upon its possession. When goods are used in stocks any one unit *conditions* only the satisfaction had from the last unit. Thus only does *marginal* utility— the actual total utility of the marginal increment — determine value. It is quite futile to attempt to distinguish between the different uses of a unit commodity and arrange these in a descending scale and choose a marginal use. When the unit is taken away all these uses would be sacrificed. Professor Dietzel, an undiscerning critic and imitator combined of the Austrians, has stated that it is the "highest use," the use on the upper margin, which determines the value of a unit commodity.[1]

A second method of discovering a marginal utility for a piano is to conceive of the utility of a piano to that possessor who has just been able to afford the price as the marginal utility of pianos. All men pay the same price for a given grade of piano, but the rich men have much higher price equivalents than the poor. If the supply of pianos to be sold in a given social market be increased, the price will fall. This fall is interpreted as being caused by a decline in the "marginal utility" of pianos. There is no justification for this logic in the utility theory. It is

---

[1] See his *Theoretische Socialökonomik*, 1895, p. 282.

not possible to compare the satisfactions had from pianos
by different persons. It is not possible to imagine the
pianos in society arranged in a series, the pianos of highest
utility being those held by the persons who could afford
to pay most and so on. The price of a piano depends
upon the *marginal price equivalent* of a piano, but neither
the exchange value nor the esteem value of a piano depends
upon *marginal* utility.

To conclude, all goods derive their exchange values from
the esteem values placed upon them by consumers. The
exchange value of a good in money is determined in a
marginal manner by the price equivalents set upon the
good by the consumers. Since the extent of a consumer's
money income helps determine the price equivalents placed
upon all articles by him, it is impossible to show that these
price equivalents depend solely upon esteem values. But
it is still proper to say that the esteem value of a good
is the sole source of its exchange value. A consumer will
assign no price equivalent to a good unless it possess
esteem value, and when he does assign a price equivalent,
it will be precisely in proportion to the esteem value of the
good as compared with other goods which he values.

The price of a commodity is a definite and fairly stable
quantity, *e. g.*, the price of an oil-stove is $4.50. Is it
possible that this definite price can be said to be determined
by the utility of oil-stoves to consumers? Consumers cannot reduce their estimates of the utility of articles directly
to figures. But, nevertheless, a consumer can determine
upon a sum of money whose general purchasing power he
considers approximately equivalent to the value of an oil-
stove to him. The value of the oil-stove is a wavering
quantity, but having struck a money estimate on the basis
of that value, taking it for what it is at the instant of the
decision, this money sum is a definite something that will be

carried in mind as such though the value is indefinite and wavering. Given these definite "price equivalents" the definite market price is a resultant from them. The market price of a good is a sort of social institution and has the momentum or stability of such an institution. Being once determined, it will not waver as do the numberless individual estimates of "esteem value" upon which it is founded.

5. If a commodity fetching a definite and exact price, as for instance an oil-stove selling for $4.50, is produced under competitive conditions, the apparent and proximate reason why the article has this particular price is because it costs its manufacturer about this sum of money to produce it. Putting aside the complications due to the fact that competition frequently takes place between firms producing at different costs, the commonest law of exchange value, stated in the usual language, is that price is "determined by" entrepreneur's cost of production. Whether entrepreneur's cost is reckoned in terms of wages, interest, and rent; wages and interest alone; or in terms merely of the prices of all the production goods "entering into" the product, the law of entrepreneur's cost, as stated above, reduces itself to the proposition that the exchange value of production goods "determines" the exchange value of products. For all forms of calculating entrepreneur's costs are based on the simple, practical, or first method of reckoning costs, as the prices of labor, raw material, machinery, power, etc.[1]

There is seeming antagonism between the law of entrepreneur's cost and the utility theory of value. For, according to the latter, the value of production goods is derived solely from the value of their products. Value

---

[1] As pointed out in section 2 of this chapter.

originates in human satisfaction, flows out to those consumption goods upon which the satisfaction is immediately
dependent (*i. e.,* by which it is conditioned), from these
flows out to the production goods upon which the consumption goods as products are dependent for their existence.   From these on, the flow of value continues to those
production goods which are still farther removed, and so on,
rank by rank, until unproduced agents are reached.   Put
in other words, raw material, machinery and similar goods,
have value solely because the entrepreneur can afford to
pay for them, and this he can do solely because his products
have value.   If value conduction runs from product to production goods, how can value determination run in the
reverse direction, from production goods to product?   If
the stream runs from the spring, we know that the volume
of the spring must determine the volume of the stream and
not the contrary.   But does not the law of entrepreneur's
cost assert that the value of production goods *determines*
the value of products?   The solution of the enigma of this
apparent conflict of the utility theory with the great empirical law of cost (in its common form of statement) is
one of the most interesting and important products of the
acute thinking of the Austrian economists.

The difficulty exists solely because many single production goods, such for example as iron and wood, or pre-
eminently common labor, enter into a variety of products.
When several various products are related to one another
by reason of the fact that a common production good
enters into all of them, we may, following von Wieser,
call them " cognate products."   If cognate products A, B,
and C are made in part from the common production good
P, P will derive its value from the values of A, B, and C,
but the value of P itself will have a peculiar reactionary

effect, yet to be described, upon the value of these products taken individually. This reaction is the phenomenon really at the foundation of the law of entrepreneur's cost. For an instant permit a supposition quite contrary to fact. Suppose that A, B, and C are made entirely from P so that no other production good enters into them. Then the exchange values of A, B, and C will be derived solely from the " marginal " utility of these products, but their exchange values are peculiar in this, that they will be related, will be adjusted, each to the others by reason of their common origin in P. If a unit of P entering into A attains in that form a higher value that when entering into B or C, then more A's will be made from P and less B's and C's. The increase in the supply of A's will decrease their value *by decreasing the marginal utility* of A's.[1] This process keeps the values of A's, B's, and C's in a mutual adjustment. If we carelessly confine our view to a part of this process of adjustment, we see what appears to be a determination of the value of A, the product, by the value of P, the production good. If the value of A is out of adjustment with its cost in P, and then the adjustment is effected, it is the value of A which seems to move to that of P. The value of P may seem to be the independently determining factor. As a matter of fact, in the first place, the value of A moves only when its marginal utility has been altered by a change of its supply, and in the second place, when it does move toward the value of P, that of P also moves toward it. It depends on the relative importance of A's in comparison with all of the rest of the products of P, how far the value of A moves and how far the value of P moves in their mutual adjustment. If it is discovered that the two stars in a

---

[1] Or at any rate, if not by decreasing their marginal utility, by decreasing their marginal price equivalent. See the section just preceding.

" double star " are approaching each other, we easily conceive that both take part in the moving.   But when an
apple falls to the earth it is more difficult to realize that the
earth also falls toward the apple, moving its due proportion
of the distance between them.   In the same way, when
we see that the value of some relatively unimportant product
remains equal to its cost of production, we are inclined to
state the case as one of pure determination of value by
cost.   But this " determination " is but a part, viewed by
itself, of a larger process by which the supplies, and consequently the values, of cognate products are being adjusted to one another.   The whole truth is that the value
of production goods is determined by the value of their
products.   Because of the existence of great common production goods of manifold productive uses, we have the
peculiar reaction of the value of production goods on the
value of products, a part of which process is described in
the law of entrepreneur's cost.

The case of real life is more complex than the one considered above in that a plurality of common production
goods always enters into a product.   In this more complex case we find an entirely new problem, which rejoices
in the name of the " imputation of the productive contribution," but the explanation of the law of entrepreneur's
cost remains exactly the same in principle as that given for
the artificially simplified case.   When a product is made
from several production goods, as a carriage from wood,
iron, leather and labor, the value which by anticipation the
production goods derive from the product is divided among
them.   The share of value of each production good is
called its productive contribution.   The different solutions
of the problem of imputing the productive contribution
already offered in the literature of value and distribution,

will not be discussed here.[1] One principle, however, will
be taken for granted. It will be assumed that the productive contribution of any kind of production good in the
value of a particular kind of product varies inversely with
the supply of this production good which is turned to the
making of that kind of product. If product A is made
from production goods P, Q and R, and the amount of
P used in producing A's is increased—with or without an
increase in the amount of Q's and R's used [2]—the productive contribution of a unit of P in the value of A's will
be decreased.

Considering now the reaction of the value of production
goods on the value of particular products, we may represent the more complex case, corresponding to real life,
by supposing products A, B and C to be made from production goods P and Q, P and R, and P and S respect-
ively. In this case the products are cognate only by reason
of their relationship through P. The production goods
Q, R and S are not common. Here as before the supplies
and values of the products A, B and C are in a relation
of mutual dependence. The dependence is, however, not
so close as in the first artificially simplified case considered
above. In the present case it is not the values of A, B
and C themselves which are brought to an equilibrium, but
it is merely the *productive contributions of P* in the values
of A, B and C that must reach an equality. If a unit of
P obtains a higher productive contribution in A than in

[1] Explanation of the principles in accordance with which the various
classes of production goods share in the value of the product is but
a part of the theory of distribution viewed in a particular way.

[2] The use of some kinds of production goods cannot be increased
without increasing to the same extent the use of certain other kinds
in the same production, but it can be shown that this does not
change the general principle of the case.

B and C, more P will be put to the making of A's and
less to the making of B's and C's, until a unit of P attains
the same productive contribution in each of these products.
If the amount of P put to the making of A's is increased,
the supply of A's will be increased and A's will decline in
value.   But the decline in the value of A's caused in this
manner will fall entirely upon the productive contribution
of P.   The decline of value takes place merely to bring
the contribution of P's in A's to an equilibrium with the
contribution of P's in B and C.   Abstract as the foregoing formulæ are, they are nevertheless real.   If entrepreneurs were not able to ascertain, at least approximately,
the productive contributions of the various production
goods entering into the product which they manufacture,
they would be unable to tell either how much of each
productive factor they can afford to buy or what price
they can pay for it.

When we call to mind the fact that in actual industry
most production goods are themselves products, and that
into the majority of final products nearly all the great
common production goods enter, we realize the stupendous
complexity of the relationships of cognate products in
actual life.   It is no wonder that ordinarily a whole half
of the process by which the values of all these fellow
products are brought to mutual adjustment escapes our
notice.   Pig iron derives its value from a thousand and
one kinds of products.   When the value of one of these
alone is being brought into adjustment with the value of
pig iron, the mass is all on the side of the pig iron, if we
may so express it.   In this movement the single product
is seeking a value-equilibrium with all the vast multitude
of other products of pig-iron.   It seems itself to effect all
the adjusting.   As a matter of fact, it contributes its due

share to the determination of the value of the raw iron. Thus far, we may safely affirm, the difficulty which, at first sight, the law of entrepreneur's cost seems to present to the utility theory has been quite surmounted.

It is a matter of some interest to define as exactly as possible the relation of potentiality cost to entrepreneur's cost. When an entrepreneur, in making his product, uses a production good capable of other applications, by other entrepreneurs, his product is made at the expense of potentiality cost. Whether in the isolated or in the social economy, there is waste whenever a good is produced at a potentiality cost which is higher than the value of the good itself. A greater value will be sacrificed to obtain a less. In the isolated economy Crusoe will easily guard himself against this form of waste. In the social economy, the competition of entrepreneurs for the supplies of production goods prevents the same form of waste. Competition being granted, nowhere will there be found an entrepreneur who uses up production goods to make a value less than the highest value that these goods could produce elsewhere. For otherwise the entrepreneurs located at the other points of higher return would be able to command the production good for their purposes, and the possibility of profits would furnish them with the motive to bid for it. If entrepreneurs' costs always consisted solely in the value of production goods capable of manifold applications, we could say that the potentiality cost of a product determined its entrepreneur's cost. For the former cost consists in the highest other values that these production goods may be made to produce elsewhere, and the entrepreneur will normally have to pay that value for them and no more. His necessary outlay for a product is thus regulated by its potentiality cost.

But sometimes in the making of a product certain valuable production goods may be used whose employment does not involve potentiality cost. These are, of course, production goods capable of being used in this one product alone. A production good may be capable of making but one kind of product and yet receive from that product a certain share of value as its productive contribution. A mineral spring may be so situated as to be such a production good. A mine is a perfect example. Here a new question confronts us. Does or does not an entrepreneur's outlay in the value of such a production good constitute a part of entrepreneur's cost? This is solely a question as to how we choose to define entrepreneur's cost. It may be defined either way. But in the event that we define this cost to include outlays for single-use production goods, it will no longer be possible to assert that potentiality cost governs entrepreneur's cost wholly and in all cases. Let us give an illustration of the question. If the bottled water of a mineral spring can sell for ten cents in a neighboring city, and it costs five cents for the bottle and labor and two cents for transportation, is or is not the three cents per bottle which remains as the rent (" price-determined surplus ") to the spring a part of the entrepreneur's cost of producing bottled mineral water? If the vender of the water did not own the spring, he would be inclined to reckon the rent paid for it to its owner as a part of his money costs. But economists are agreed that the distinction between costs and surpluses does not hinge on relations of legal ownership. If the producer of the bottled water owned the spring, he would merely pay the rent of it to himself. To the present writer it seems that entrepreneur's cost may be defined either to be coextensive with potentiality cost, or to exceed this cost by the inclusion of

" price-determined " rents,[1] provided a consistent usage be
maintained.   In the one case, entrepreneur's cost is determined by potentiality cost; in the other case it is principally
determined by potentiality cost.[2]

[1] When a single-use production good is short-lived instead of durable, so that it receives its value from its product in one payment, instead of a series of payments in time, we do not call its value return
a " rent." Its value is nevertheless " price-determined " in the same
sense as the rents just discussed and belongs to the same category as
these rents.
   The term " price-determined rent " has, among professed followers
of Ricardo (such as Professor Marshall who holds to Ricardo's theory
in the main), come to mean the income to a durable single-use production good. In the most unfortunate terminology of the Ricardian
school—which the writer believes can be traced back to their ultimately false philosophy of value—a " price-determined rent " is one
which " does not enter into price." But the leading exponents of
present-day Ricardian doctrine are now agreed, it seems, that when a
production good is capable of more than one application—as land to
wheat or fruit or pasture—its rent *does enter* into the price of its
product. Therefore they mean by a price-determined rent, not the
rent of such a good, but the rent of a single-use production good.

[2] A plausible argument could be made to show that we have Ricardo's
authority for maintaining that price-determined rents must not be
considered a part of entrepreneur's cost. For Ricardo said " rent cannot enter in the least degree into price." But there can be no question that by this he meant that rent cannot enter into cost of production. As was frequent with him, he did not say precisely what he
meant. Malthus had said that cost of production includes wages, " profits," and rent, and that profits and rent, not being paid for labor, pre-
vented the regulation of value by pure labor cost. Ricardo admitted
that profits enter into cost but minimized the difficulty thus granted in
the labor theory. On the contrary he denied that rent enters into cost.
The first paragraph of his chapter on rent shows it to be his purpose in
that chapter to justify this denial. Later he stated his contention as
being that rent cannot enter into " price," instead of cost.
   Now Ricardo frequently thought of cost as being composed of
" labour and profits " ! In most places we can make his reasonings
clear only by substituting for this hybrid concept a plain concept of
entrepreneur's cost If Ricardo habitually meant entrepreneur's cost
by the words " cost of production," then his famous doctrine comes to

In accounting for the value of consumption goods the Austrian theory takes their supply for granted. In the same way, when the Austrians come to their explanation of the law of cost they take the supplies of production goods for granted. If the supply of pig iron brought every year to the iron market be increased, the supply of the products of iron will be increased and the exchange values of these products will fall. The exchange value of pig iron will fall in consequence.[1] At this point a question—a criticism in behalf of the cost theories of value— naturally suggests itself. Is not supply ultimately regulated by cost of production in some form, and is not cost of production thus either the ultimate regulator of value itself, or at least a joint regulator with utility? We have suggested here the famous question of the " reconciliation " of the cost and the utility theories of value. It is certain that the only form of cost which can exercise ultimate control over the supply of any produced good is what we have called by the generic name of " pain cost." The potentiality cost of a product is measured in the value of the production goods entering it. But this value itself depends on the supply of these production goods. The ultimate cost regulator of the value of both the products and the production goods cannot be potentiality cost. The influence of potentiality cost causes the supply of the in-

---

signify that price-determined rents are not properly a part of entrepreneur's costs. As far as the present writer can see, our decision in this regard is purely a matter of arbitrary choice between two possible definitions of entrepreneur's cost. As far as Ricardo is concerned, he had no clear and definite concept or concepts of cost. Into *potentiality cost*, a price-determined rent assuredly does not enter.

[1] The value of the iron may fall earlier in time than the value of its products, because entrepreneurs using it know beforehand that the increased products of pig will have to be sold lower.

dividual kind of product merely to be adjusted to the supplies of its cognate products. But potentiality cost has no influence whatever over the total supply of the production goods or the absolute supply of the total mass of cognate products. To appeal to a simple illustration, if a flow or stream of some production good be supposed to divide into several branches as it proceeds, each branch representing one of the several cognate products of that good, the influence of potentiality cost may determine the *relative volumes of the different product-streams,* but only pain cost—if any cost at all—can influence the volume of the parent stream, and thus govern the *absolute volume of all the branches.* Entrepreneur's cost also, most obviously, fails as an ultimate regulator of supply. This cost is but the proximate agency through which the two elementary forms of cost exert their influences upon the relative and absolute supplies of products. Undoubtedly the recognition that pain cost is the only form of cost capable of exerting any ultimate control of value, helps to suggest that it be called " real cost " or " true cost." Professor Marshall, for instance, analyzes cost into two forms, (1) real, and (2) money costs.

6. There is to-day a large following for the doctrine that cost and utility are joint and equal regulators of value. Professor Alfred Marshall, for instance, states that " we might as reasonably dispute whether it is the upper or the under blade of a pair of scissors that cuts a piece of paper, as whether value is governed by utility or cost of production." [1] Historically, there have been developed by economists two distinct and apparently antagonistic theories professing to afford ultimate explanations of value; the earlier or cost and the later or utility theory. But if it

[1] *Principles of Economics,* 4th ed., 1898, p. 428.

can be shown that in reality cost and utility are but joint regulators of value, recent thinkers hold this equivalent to a demonstration that the two apparently hostile doctrines are after all but the two parts of a larger harmonious whole.	It is, therefore, maintained by many that the two opposed schools of value merely failed to take a broad enough view of the problem.	Thus we have ever before us the interesting question of the reconciliation of the cost and utility theories.	If it be desired to effect a fundamental reconciliation, what appears to be the most propitious starting point is found in the theory of the " marginal or final equivalence of utility and disutility," a doctrine which originates purely as a theory of " subjective " or esteem value in contrast with exchange value.	The first writer to give this theory a definite formulation was probably Gossen, but it was J. B. Clark's later but entirely independent statement of the same idea which was first to bring it to the notice of economists generally.[1]

Professor Clark develops a theory that the ultimate standard of the value of a good is the " effective social disutility " cost of its acquisition.	Thus he presents a theory of distinctively social valuation.[2]	But we also find as a part of his doctrines a theory of purely individual valuations.	Professor Clark distinguishes clearly between these two, and in fact develops the theory of social from the theory of individual valuation.	In drawing the reader's attention to these doctrines, it will suit our purposes best

[1] Professor Clark's theory appeared first in the *New Englander* for 1881. Gossen's statement of the same fundamental idea was much earlier, but the strange fate of his work is known to all. Professor Clark's theory of value was developed by him independently of Gossen and of Menger and Jevons as well.

[2] See the *Distribution of Wealth,* chap. xxiv.

to emphasize as much as possible the distinction between value in the individual economy and in the social economy. We may, therefore, adopt the device of " Crusoe economics," and consider the relation of subjective cost to value in the isolated individual economy. In the theory of value, the pursuit of this plan does not involve a waste of time, but on the contrary it is an excellent measure for which there is precedent at some point or other in the writings of nearly all theorists. The plan corresponds to the artifice of the primitive society of hunters and fishers so frequently used and also abused by the classical economists. It is in a peculiar degree a device of what Roscher called the " idealistic method." We are, of course, now dealing with a problem entirely outside the possible sphere of the " historical method." We find in the Crusoe economy the prototype, as it were, of many a complex value relation in advanced social conditions, and an appreciation of certain simple and highly generalized principles true of this economy may greatly facilitate our understanding of the difficult subject of cost and value under real conditions. But the strongest reason of all for considering consciously and explicitly the case of Crusoe by himself, is because there are many examples in the literature of value where certain doctrines are laid down ostensibly as universal principles, which are in reality conditioned upon the unconscious assumption of Crusoe conditions. The case of Crusoe should be discussed if only to show what principles are limited to the conditions of his economy.

Crusoe might possess various articles of value which cost him no labor, or cost him an entirely negligible amount, such as certain scarce fruits; but the major part of Crusoe's wealth, let us. suppose, is produced, and is freely reproducible, by his labor. The amount of labor power which he expends upon his island is variable at his pleasure within

wide limits. If he choose to work only a few hours a
day through the year, he will produce only a certain limited
amount of the most useful things. If he add more hours
per day, he will produce more of the old kinds of goods
and also other different articles, luxuries as contrasted with
necessities, but at any rate things of lower utility. Thus
as Crusoe increases the hours of labor power put forth
per day, he finds that there is a decline in the additional
utility produced by each successive increment of labor. On
the other hand, he finds that the pain cost or disutility
of labor increases as he toils longer and longer. Crusoe
will, for his average day, work until the increasing disutility
of labor comes to an equality in his judgment with the
decreasing utility of the things being produced. It would
not be rational for him to stop at an earlier point, for then
further labor would produce him a means of satisfaction
greater than the " pain " of the labor itself. Nor would
he labor beyond this point so that the pain would exceed
the pleasure gain. Thus the utility produced by, and the
disutility of, the final increment of labor in the working-
day counterbalance, or we have the " marginal equivalence
of utility and disutility."

The most important part of Professor Clark's teaching
is that the disutility of labor expended in producing goods
is the ultimate standard of their value. To establish this
thesis, it is necessary for him to show that the " effective "
disutility of an increment of labor is always the actual disutility of the final increment, and that the " effective "
utility produced by any increment is the actual utility produced by the final increment. If Crusoe works ten hours
a day, any hour of the day's labor will have the same
effective disutility as the tenth hour. Thus if it costs one
hour of labor to produce the article A, the pain cost of
A is always *in effect* the disutility of the final or tenth

hour of labor, no matter in what part of the day the good A happens actually to be produced. For if Crusoe should decide to go without this article in order to avoid the hour of labor which it costs, his day would then consist of nine hours spent upon the rest of his products, and the effect would be to save himself the disutility of the tenth or last hour.[1] By shortening the working-day an hour he cannot do otherwise than save himself from suffering this marginal disutility.

In a similar way it can be shown that the *effective* utility of a product A produced by the first hour of labor is the same as the actual utility of the product B produced by the tenth hour. For if A were to be lost, destroyed, or traded away, another A could be produced in its stead through the sacrifice of a B, by turning the tenth hour from B to the production of an A. In effect, then, upon the possession of A is *dependent* merely the utility of B. The utility of a good is defined as its power to afford satisfaction, but the " effective utility " of a good as conceived by Professor Clark is, we may say, the power of that good over a man's satisfactions, taking into consideration the adjustments he may make in his productive activities in case of the loss of that good. If he produces this same good over again, and instead goes without some other good, *in effect* he foregoes the utility of the latter, and this is precisely the *effective utility* of the first good.[2] Thus, in

---

[1] So large an increment as an hour is taken merely as a matter of convenience. There is a certain form of attack upon all marginal methods of theorizing in economics which is always met by making the increments infinitesimal. It is hardly necessary to guard against that attack here.

[2] The curious reader would find it of interest to compare Professor Smart's statement that the value of a good is almost always in the end measured by a " foreign utility." " The value of a horse may be

Professor Clark's view, the utility produced by the last increment of a man's labor affords a unit for measuring the effective utility to him of any and all the freely producible products of his labor. But it has already been shown that the *disutility* of this last increment of labor is equal to the utility produced by it. Thus terminal disutility becomes also an available unit of "subjective" or esteem value, and Professor Clark adopts this as the "ultimate standard of value" upon the ground that pain is a more convenient measure than pleasure.[1] The theory signifies that the subjective value to the isolated producer of any good whose supply depends on labor can be most conveniently measured by the labor cost of that good. To quote:

It follows that, in the case of an isolated man, we may measure the subjective value of goods by the mere duration of the work that creates them. All goods made in an hour are equal in effective utility and all hours of labor are of equal effective disutility. Destroy the product of an hour's work, and you injure the man by a fixed amount; make any hour's work unnecessary, by making nature freely supply what is produced in that period, and you benefit the man by a fixed amount . . . The product of two hours' work will always be of just twice as much subjective value as is the product of one.[2]

Professor Clark has in some place defined subjective value as the "measure of effective utility." Menger defined this

measured by the foreign utility of a summer vacation." See *Introduction to the Theory of Value*, pp. 37-8. Much dialectical exercise of interest could be had by comparing fully the precise formulæ of "marginal" utility developed by the Austrian economists and Prof. Clark's formula. Clark's theory is at bottom in harmony with the Austrian, but goes further.

[1] See *op. cit.*, p. 380.   [2] *Ibid.* p. 389.

kind of value as the significance attained by a good in our estimation when we know that some satisfaction of ours is conditioned upon command of this particular good. Value, as an amount, is the measure of the quantity of satisfaction conditioned. The present writer has already expressed his opinion [1] that Menger's mere definition of value gives the solution to the great riddle of the relation of value to usefulness and satisfaction, and that virtually from the mere proposition contained in this definition a large part of the theory of value can be deduced directly. It is of great interest to note, therefore, that Professor Clark's definition of subjective value is in entire harmony with Menger's. The definition of Menger explains value universally, wherever there is value. Clark's definition, though conceived quite independently by him, is but an extension of the principle in Menger's definition, but an application of it to a certain special case. This case, though logically a special instance, is however typical of most of the goods we imagine a Crusoe to be producing, consuming and reproducing. This is the case of freely reproducible goods. Here, if a good be destroyed, its value will be revealed by the satisfaction that must be given up because of its destruction, which is the satisfaction finally conditioned upon it. In the end, what Professor Clark points out is merely that this good may be replaced by diverting to its making labor which otherwise would have been employed in producing some other good which Crusoe chooses to resign instead. The satisfaction in effect, or in the end, conditioned by good A is the satisfaction directly conditioned by or afforded by good B, the good given up. [2]

---

[1] *Cf. ante* p. 145.

[2] A brief comparison of the Austrian concept of " marginal utility " with Clark's concept of " effective utility " may be of interest. Many

As it appears to the present writer, Clark's theory of esteem value is to this point so well founded that even the most uncompromising opponent of labor theories can find no ground to deny it. We have here explained a labor measure of esteem value, perfectly justified at least under the conditions of the isolated economy, and Professor Clark's analysis has disclosed the inner reasons why this measure can be employed. Indeed, while speaking of reproducible goods in the Crusoe economy, it may be affirmed that cost is not only a " measure " of esteem value, but is also a joint *regulator* of value. To be precise, the costliness of a good acts jointly with the utility of the good in regulating its value. To say that one thing regulates another is, of course, asserting more than that it measures

kinds of goods are divisible into parts without changing their economic nature. Grain is a good example. A piano is an example of the other kind of good, the unit good. When a given good is divisible into increments, the Austrians point out that the value of any or every increment depends purely upon the satisfaction afforded by the last used or least useful increment. Putting it in another way, they say the marginal utility of the good is the actual utility of the last increment, and value depends on marginal utility. The very essence of this principle is that the value of a thing, as for instance first increment, does not depend on its own exact utility. Professor Clark, developing his thought in his own way, and using a different terminology, goes further than the Austrians, but along the same line. The " effective " utility of a good is not its own utility, but is that other least utility produced by the same amount of labor. The Austrians state that the value of any bushel of wheat depends on the utility of the " last " bushel, because if any bushel is removed the result will be that the last bushel is really given up, or any bushel is in effect the last. Clark points out that among goods which are all freely reproducible, the value of the product of any unit of labor time depends on the utility of the least useful product produced by a unit of labor time, though this other least useful product be an entirely different kind of good and not an increment of the same kind of good. Many minute questions in this connection we may pass for lack of space.

stliness of this grain should fall, its value woul
wered, for Crusoe would be led to produce mor
rder to reach the point of supply which equili
l cost and satisfaction. Thus the marginal util
lue would be lowered. Conversely if the costli-
ncreased, value will be raised. Under Crusoe
we are considering the relations of costliness,
d value in the simplest of circumstances we can
Even here the question arises, is it correct to
t costliness is *precisely coördinate* with utility in
ng value? To me it seems apparent that utility
a more direct and intimate control over value
, even in the simplified case now before us.[1] In
place, value is still *derived* solely from utility.[2]
uences value only by way of influencing the value-
ing utility itself. Thus cost is more remote from
an is satisfaction or utility. Even in the case of
lued according to their "effective utility," that is,
g to a foreign utility, there is no violation of the
that value is derived solely from utility. Cost or
ss is never the source of value. No amount of
lured for a good without utility will confer value
There can be no discrepancy between utility (here
speaking of the utility that is the counterpart of the
tion *conditioned* upon the good, *i. e.*, the marginal
in the cases of goods divisible into increments) and
whereas there may be between costliness and value.
thing prevents the supply of a good from being

ons will appear later, it is believed, to show that when we
e complex case of real social industry and exchange value
trol of cost over value will be much more impaired than
utility.
as already been shown why it is quite impossible to hold to
ion that cost is the essence of value. *Cf. ante* pp. 34-5.

that other. A regulator is a measuring cause, whereas a mere measure is not a cause of the thing estimated.[1]

In what precise sense is costliness here a co-determinant of value? When a good both costs pain or discomfort in its production and affords pleasure in its use, it is common custom to speak of the " cost " of the good as the exact opposite of its " utility." But these concepts are not direct opposites. Cost consists in the subjective experiences of

[1] Without attempting a systematic classification of kinds of causes, we all know that such is our notion of cause that we can conceive of many causes which bear no assignable quantitative relation with their effects (*i. e.*, effects for which they are partly responsible). The pressure of an electric button " caused " the Hell Gate explosion (after conditions—*i. e.*, other causes—were prepared) but the amount of pressure put upon this button, or the size of this button, had nothing to do with the quantity of the explosion or the amount of work done in the explosion. We are permitted to speak of the act of pressing the button as a cause, but not as a regulator (except with respect to the *time* of the explosion, an irrelevant consideration here), for a regulator is a cause the quantity of which determines the quantity of the effect. It should be noted that when the quantity of the cause is compared with the quantity of the effect, to show that the former regulates the latter, the quantity of the cause must be established independently of the quantity of this same effect; otherwise the fallacy of reasoning in a circle is committed. This digression does not lead us so far astray from the theory of value as might be supposed. This precise fallacy has been committed time and again in the reasonings that have been brought to the support of the labor theory of value. For instance when the term "labor" is used to signify disutility or cost (instead of productive power) by the expounders of the "difficulty of attainment" philosophy of value, and it is asserted that the labor cost of a good regulates its value, the objection is soon encountered that skilled labor produces a greater value per day than common. Thereupon it is frequently explained that skilled labor is condensed, or counts as more labor per day than common. As a matter of fact, we all know that in the vast majority of cases, skilled labor, measured independently of the value produced by it, and measured as a quantity of labor in the sense of disutility, is less labor per day than common toil.

the producing man, and its precise opposite is pleasure or, specifically in our economic usage, satisfaction of want. But " utility " never is a precise equivalent for satisfaction. On the contrary, utility is another kind of opposite of satisfaction, being always conceived to belong to the good and not to lie within the man, except in the treatises of certain unconscious metaphysicians. In virtue of a certain combination of physical properties a good possesses a power to produce a satisfaction in a man.[1] This power, due to its physical properties, is the best conception of the good's utility. The precise opposite of utility cannot be designated by cost, but the word " costliness " fits the need. In virtue of their physical properties, or physical and chemical relations with other external things, some goods require a large amount of change of man's external surroundings to be effected by him in order that they may be produced. We give these goods the attribute of costliness, similar to the attribute of utility, and the relation

---

[1] Whenever, of course, the man acting for himself, places himself in the relation with the good which permits its power to become effective. Compare the discussion in section ii of this chapter. No apology is offered for the present " discussion of mere words " as it might be termed by the hostile. These discussions contribute to clearness of thought upon questions of theory, and clearness of thought in theory is certain from time to time to be of benefit to discussions of many proximate and practical issues. For instance, we find recently a well known writer explaining that " scientifically " the distribution of money among nations is so governed that money reaches the level of equal " marginal utility " in the different countries. See a paper entitled " The Distribution of Money," *Journal of Political Economy,* vol. ix, p. 49. This proposition has no meaning, and is authorized by nothing in the Austrian theory, though the writer quotes the Austrians freely. A little " word discussion " by " practical " writers might enable them to see when they are covering up the absence of an explanation by mere conjuring with formulæ whose real meaning has not been ascertained.

---

between costliness and
tween utility and satisf

The question which
case of freely producibl
be augmented at will b
the costliness of a good
in determining its value
good determines its value
creature of the supply of
the lower the marginal
way it is often stated in
that will be produced dep
and thus at bottom cost de
careful statement we may s
both the costliness and th
crease the supply—the *aver*
if speaking of a crop—un
ginal satisfaction become eq
the increase of the number
entail an increase of margin
ginal utility. Both the ma
utility vary when the suppl
tends to rest at the point of
tities, and is thus determine

---

[1] The term " disutility " is almos
" discomfort," that is, as being
available as an opposite of satisfact
usage of those writers who use the
same usage debars its employment
sense advocated in the present essay.

[2] The determination of Crusoe's su
fixes the subjective value of the goo
to the determination of competitive
market at the point of " normal equ
as described by Professor Marshall.

general co
soon be lo
of it in
brates fina
ity and v
ness be
condition
utility an
imagine.
affirm tha
determini
exercises
than cos
the first
Cost infl
determin
value th
goods v
accordin
principl
costlines
cost en
upon it.
we are
satisfac
utility
value,
If any

[1] Rea
reach t
the con
that of
[2] It
the opi

increased to the point of marginal equivalence of utility and costliness, then of course the value follows the utility and not the costliness. Costliness is thus not a more fundamental cause of value, but merely a more remote cause than utility, and in any event can influence value only by affecting the utility itself, by helping to determine supply.

7. Turning to social conditions, we meet the new problem of exchange value. It is true, certain value comparisons may be made in the entirely isolated economy which afford a kind of prototype of the exchange value of the market. Crusoe might, perhaps, have occasion to make mental note that ten bushels of his wheat supply possess the same esteem value to him as one cord of his firewood. This comparison involves a ratio between valuable goods, and if Crusoe only had reason to trade with himself we might find the phenomenon of purchasing power—the true conception of exchange value—and ten bushels of wheat would have the purchasing power of one cord of wood. This kind of exchange value—if we dare call it such—would be most simple; for it would be directly determined by, and be in exact proportion to, esteem value. Just as Crusoe will be able to carry the esteem values of reproducible goods in mind most readily in terms of disutility cost, so would he be able to strike value ratios between such goods most easily by comparing the disutility costs of their physical units of measure. Thus, if one cord of wood should exchange for ten bushels of wheat, the reason would be that a bushel of wheat costs one-tenth as much labor as one cord of wood. This thought need not be pursued further. If the exchange value of a good in the social market depended in the same direct manner upon the esteem value of that good to all society or to " society as a unit," the final theory of exchange value would be much simplified. But, unless the present writer is mistaken, a good

cannot possess an esteem value to society as a whole, but can merely have a separate value to each individual member of society.

Though it is questionable whether we can apply the theory of final equivalence of utility and disutility directly and in an unmodified form to all kinds of social value, we still find generally that each individual in society values his personal consumption goods substantially in the same manner as Crusoe. Under the division of labor, the individual does not produce his own consumption goods, but renders certain productive services to society for which he receives remuneration in the shape of a money income. Money income may also be derived from capital acquired at the cost of abstinence on the part of the individual receiving it. But again, it may as well be the result of gift or inheritance, in which case it represents no subjective cost to the recipient. When a dollar costs a man subjective sacrifice to acquire it, and the dollar is spent for a commodity, this commodity thus indirectly costs that sacrifice. The commodity is bought by the consumer because it possesses esteem value. It derives this esteem value from the satisfaction conditioned by it, but this value may well be carried in mind by the consumer in terms of his own subjective cost. Crusoe spends units of disutility, as it were, to obtain from nature certain utilities; the man under social conditions spends dollars, which may represent disutility, to obtain utilities from the social warehouse. Professor Clark's theory of " effective disutility " as the measure of value may be applied to the individual economy within society as well as to the individual economy in isolation.

Everywhere in society among individuals who earn a part or all of their money incomes,[1] we may expect to find

---

[1] A man may receive part of his income by gift or inheritance and

pure " esteem values " being measured by subjective costs.
But the relation of subjective cost to *exchange value* is a
different matter.   Two parlor tables of the same make and
pattern will possess the same exchange values, but the
esteem values of the two to their separate owners are not
comparable quantities.   Each of these owners, for himself,
may estimate the esteem value of the table in terms of its
indirect *cost of acquisition* in his own disutility.   The dollars cost him disutility and the table cost him dollars.   But
this is not at all the same as saying that the " exchange
value " of a table is measured by the disutility *cost of production* of that commodity.   Exchange value can have no
such intimate relation with disutility cost as esteem value.
Furthermore, the cost of production of tables is experienced only by makers of tables, and not by their consumers.
The exchange values and pain costs of commodities can
have no closer relation than one of mere proportionality.
It is possible that, if one A has an exchange value of two
B, an A has cost twice as much disutility to produce as
a B.   In this case the exchange values of these commodities, each in terms of the other, are proportional to their
subjective costs.   It is permissible to predicate equality of
subjective cost and esteem value, but to say that the subjective cost of an article *equals* its exchange value would,
of course, convey no meaning.   The unqualified classical
labor theory asserted that exchange values were determined
in proportion to relative labor costs.   The aim of this chap-

earn a part. The latter part becomes in this case a sort of marginal
portion. Though all of his dollars have not cost him disutility, some
of them have, and upon principles already discussed, any dollar has
the "effective" disutility cost of the most costly dollars. This is
just as true as the fact that the first hours of labor may sometimes be
play and yet their product always counts as having a disutility cost
because of the disutility of the final hour.

ter has been, therefore, to prepare to answer this question: Are the exchange values of commodities in the social market in proportion to the subjective costs of production of these commodities? Is there any way of defining, or method of reckoning, the pain cost of a good, which will enable us to show this proportionality?

Before attending directly to these questions, it is best to consider whether it is possible to compare the subjective costs of commodities produced by different persons or groups of persons. A ton of coal may exchange for six bushels of wheat. The subjective cost of the coal consists chiefly in the labor of certain miners; that of the wheat in the labor of certain farmers. To assert that the subjective costs of production of these commodities either are or are not in proportion to their respective exchange values, implies that we are able to compare these costs as quantities. To assert proportionality requires that we be able to say that the disutility experienced by the miners in producing a ton of coal is equal to that experienced by the farmers in producing six bushels of wheat. To assert disproportionality, we must be able to state that these disutilities are unequal. If these disutilities are quite incommensurable, we can assert nothing regarding the relation of these costs to the corresponding exchange values.[1] Men as scholars are accustomed to maintain that the pleasures or pains of different minds cannot be compared as quantities, while in every-day life the same men are equally accustomed to state that John *enjoys* music *more* than Paul, or that Primus *suffers more* or works *harder* than Secundus. May or may

---

[1] The reader should bear in mind that the "theory of price," in which exchange value is explained according to the utility theory of value, involves so comparison whatever of the satisfactions of different persons. See *ante*, § 4.

not we affirm that the stoker works harder, or in our own
jargon, suffers more disutility, than the dining-room steward? In the hope of settling part of the issues raised in
these questions, let us consider the meaning of one of
Adam Smith's statements regarding wages in different employments. I refer to the doctrine that wages tend to be
higher than the average in employments where there is a
higher degree of disutility. This tendency is operative
only under perfect competition, and the existence of numerous non-competing groups occasions a result much changed
from that to be expected from this tendency, which is
sometimes described in the " evil paradox " that the harder
the work, the lower the wages. The question which con-
cerns us here is, how much does either of the above statements imply with respect to the possibility of comparing
the pains or pleasures of different persons. It seems to the
writer that neither necessitates a direct quantitative comparison of the subjective experiences of different persons.
I may, perhaps, say that the persons in occupation A are
suffering more disutility and receiving higher wages than
those in employment B, but all I can be supposed really to
know is that if I were in occupation A, I would suffer
more discomfort than if I were in occupation B. If I am
a person of " average " (*i. e.,* typical) constitution, I may
infer legitimately that this is true also of any average person. While making no affirmation that John suffers more
disutility than Paul, either when these persons are in the
same or in different employments;[1] we may be able to state
that either John or Paul will suffer more in occupation A
than in B. The upshot of the matter is that Adam Smith's
proposition implies only our ability to compare the *dis-*

[1] This kind of affirmation is, however, very common, and hence the
presumption is that it has a legitimate meaning.

utility (using this word in the sense it ought to have) of
different tasks. A task is objective, consisting in certain
objective results to be effected under certain objective conditions. When the objective characteristics of a task necessitate subjective discomfort in the person who performs it,
the task or employment possesses *disutility,* which is thus
a concept the opposite of *utility.* If within a competing
group employment A affords a higher wage than employment B, because its *disutility* is higher, the result is brought
about not, in the first instance, through the perception by
the workers that certain individual persons work harder
than other individual persons, but through the perception
that any normal individual for himself would work harder
at the task A than at the task B. The possibility of comparison is implied merely between the " pains " of the same
person, though there are common.forms of expression which
imply more. We may conclude, then, that there is a perfectly legitimate sense in which we can compare the subjective costliness of commodities produced in society by
entirely different groups of persons. And no one doubts
that the day's product of a coal miner has a higher disutility cost than the day's product of a farmer.

When we find the statement in an economic treatise that
the exchange values of commodities are ultimately regulated by their subjective cost, it is to be assumed that the
meaning is the same as that which would be expressed
with greater precision by using the word costliness. With
the explanations already offered we may henceforth follow
common usage and employ the mere word cost. There are
two distinct ways of reckoning the pain cost of a commodity, namely, (1) as total cost; (2) as marginal cost.
Ricardo reckoned cost according to a hybrid method. The
total subjective cost of a good consists in all the discomforts of labor and abstinence actually endured in the past

to produce it. Taking the factor of labor alone for illustration, it includes the cost of the labor directly applied to the good, and of the labor indirectly applied by being directly applied to the raw material and machinery which are used up in its making. The machinery, however, has always been made at the combined expense of labor and of using up formerly existing tools and machinery; and the latter tools and machines had a labor cost. A product's total cost may include, perhaps, one one-hundredth of the labor cost of the first generation of certain machinery used in its production, and as we go back, one one-millionth of the second generation;[1] and the total labor cost of any commodity thus goes back no man knows how far. Therefore, the total labor cost alone of a good (to say nothing of the abstinence element) is an extremely indefinite quantity; and it is impossible to know anything very definite about the comparative total labor costs of different articles. But beyond this, we do know that the existence of differential rents destroys the possibility of proportionality between total labor costs and exchange values.

The concept of the *marginal cost* of a good appears in the Ricardian theory of rent, and has been involved more or less clearly in the reasonings of most modern economists, but it is almost entirely to J. B. Clark that we owe the consistent development of this idea. The marginal

---

[1] Suppose a machine is destroyed in the making of 100 units of a certain product.. Then the total labor cost of each of these units contains $\frac{1}{100}$ of the total labor cost of this machine. This is explained by Ricardo and by recent followers of Ricardo, as for instance by Professor Macvane in his text book. Another earlier machine was partly used up in making this first one. Perhaps it contributed $\frac{1}{10000}$ of its total labor cost to this first. Then each of our products contains in its total labor cost $\frac{1}{100}$ of $\frac{1}{10000}$ of the total labor cost of the machine of the second generation back.

subjective cost of a good may consist either of labor or of abstinence, but not of both combined. In this essay we will arbitrarily set aside the problem of abstinence cost. The marginal labor cost of a good is, of course, determined by ascertaining the marginal product of labor in producing this good. To illustrate in the simplest manner possible, we will follow the time-honored procedure of eliminating capital for the moment, and suppose successive doses of labor to be applied to a given piece of land.[1] Let the labor force applied stand at a certain amount, and suppose the dose to consist of a labor day. Then, if experimentation reveals the fact that the addition of one more dose will increase the whole product by the amount of two bushels, we define these two bushels to be the marginal product of a labor day. Professor Clark frequently refers to this same quantum as the *specific* product of labor. The land in this case may have consisted of a 100-acre field and the total labor applied may have amounted to, say, 300 labor days. The total produce may have been 3,000 bushels of grain. By hypothesis, capital being eliminated, the total labor cost of these 3,000 bushels is 300 labor days, or ten bushels cost one labor day, or the total cost of a bushel is one-tenth of a day. On the other hand, the marginal cost of a bushel is one-half of a labor day, since two bushels are the marginal product of a day.[2]

[1] Using capital here in the sense of means of production that are themselves products of labor. We will go so far in our illustration as to suppose that the land has never had labor expended upon it to drain it, or in any other way to "fix an element of capital in it."

[2] In this illustration the marginal cost is five times as high as the "total cost" or total average cost of a bushel, but this ratio could have no significance even if the data of our illustration were approximately true with respect to the *direct* labor cost of wheat on good land, for we have eliminated from the real total labor cost all of what Ricardo called the "indirect" labor cost, by eliminating capital.

Ricardo, who so explicitly defined total labor cost as consisting of the labor both directly and indirectly applied to a commodity, also assumed that in one respect value-determining cost is *marginal,* though he never used the word "marginal." It was for this reason that not far back we described his method of defining cost as hybrid. His doctrine that rent does not enter into cost was but one way of stating that *on land,* it is only marginal cost (as he expressed it, the cost of the most costly portion of the supply) which determines value. In real life, products are the result of combining not land and labor alone, but land, labor and capital (in the sense excluding land—our usage at present). When Ricardo was expounding and illustrating the theory of rent which bears his name, he was forced to suppose that the successive doses added to land were composed of capital and labor jointly,[1] which left his marginal quantum the product of both of these agents. This left him with the great interest difficulty with which he occupied himself in his first chapter.[2] It remained for J. B. Clark to point out that the marginal product of labor could be disentangled from the product of capital as well as from that of land.[3] Upon this possibility depends the important productivity theory of wages. In order to explain the process by which the pure marginal product of labor is found by the entrepreneur, Clark adopts what is virtually the business man's conception of capital,

[1] Ricardo frequently supposed his doses to consist of sums of money expended by the farmer, or to consist of increments of money capital. These doses of money, however, would be expended for capital goods and labor power conjointly.

[2] Traced in the fifth chapter of the present essay.

[3] That is to say, when we affirm that in our theory we can disentangle the specific product of labor, we mean that entrepreneurs in practical effect do ascertain the marginal product of labor in making up their labor forces.

as distinguished from concrete capital goods. The latter
alone have been designated capital by most economists in
their formal and explicit definitions. Professor Clark prefers to call the two concepts simply capital [1] and capital
goods. Capital is a "sum of productive wealth, invested
in material things which are perpetually shifting—which
come and go continually — although the fund abides." [2]
These material things are the capital goods. Capital as
an amount must be measured by its exchange value. A
capital of $100,000 may be prepared to employ say 40 men.
Should it be rearranged to employ 20 men, its concrete
make-up would have to be altered. A less number of
machines and tools of better quality would have to compose it. Now as the concrete tissue of a given capital
perishes or matures and frees its value for reinvestment in
more concrete goods, an entrepreneur has it open to him
to alter the concrete constitution of his capital. In this
way, in the course of time, an entrepreneur may be able to
rearrange his capital so as to augment or decrease the
labor force employed with it. In many cases pretty large
changes in the labor supply employed with a given capital
could be made with little or no alteration of its technical
concrete make-up. Somewhat slowly and under this and
that frictional difficulty, the experimentation is made which
reveals the marginal product of labor. The process which
discloses this must always in the end be one in which an
increment of labor is added to or removed from the force
working with a given capital and an observation made
of the resulting addition to or subtraction from the total
product. The exposition of this process and the explanation why competition tends to make the wages of labor
(of whatever grade) equal to its specific or marginal prod-

---

[1] Sometimes "pure capital."   [2] *Distribution of Wealth*, p. 119.

uct, is probably the greatest contribution to economics contained in Clark's *Distribution to Wealth,* and occupies a large part of that work.

As was virtually pointed out by Malthus,[1] the presence of rent and interest charges in entrepreneur's costs is an insuperable obstacle in the way of the theory that a commodity's total labor cost is proportionate to its exchange value. If, however, an attempt is made to correlate *marginal* labor cost and exchange value, the difficulties of rent and interest are eliminated. When we say that these difficulties are eliminated, we do not mean that they are arbitrarily set aside, or that we merely run away from them: but the marginal labor cost of a commodity is not affected by the payment of rent and interest. For instance, if wheat is being produced at the same time on land of the best and land of the poorest grade, a large rent will be paid out of the total wheat product on the former soil, and little or no rent may be paid out of the total product on the latter, and yet the cultivation will be carried to the point which makes the marginal product of labor and the marginal labor cost of wheat the same on both grades. The same observations may be applied to rent of capital (or interest, as we call it when it is calculated as a percentage of the value of the rent-bearing agent).[2]

The great difficulty in the way of the theorem that the marginal labor costs of commodities are in proportion[3] to their exchange values, is the problem of skilled labor. The best way to show the effect of skilled labor upon com-

---

[1] See *ante,* chap. vii, § § 4 and 5.

[2] Adopting the view of the income of capital taken by Professor Clark and advocated with so much force by Professor F. A. Fetter.

[3] By this phrase we mean always *in relative proportion,* so that the value of A is to that of B, as the cost of A is to that of B.

parative marginal costs is first to eliminate it temporarily from the problem, and show what the relation of marginal labor cost would be to exchange value, if there were only common labor throughout society. If all labor were of a single grade, all commodities which are products of labor would have exchange values in proportion to their respective marginal disutility costs. This would be true whether the products are consumption goods or are merely production goods which are used in making further products. Some valuable goods are not products of labor. Such are bodies of ore lying in their natural state, standing timber, *etc.* These production goods have no disutility cost, marginal or total, and consequently their exchange values have no relation to cost. Their supplies are determined independently of human agency. Ore at the surface, crushed or smelted ore, are, however, products of labor, and so long as only a part of the known existing ore of mines is removed—a part remaining untouched because of too high cost—the supply of any product resulting from the combination of labor and native ore-bodies, will depend upon marginal labor cost.[1]

The homogeneous labor force (which we have assumed temporarily) will distribute itself among all the various industries in society in proportions determined by the marginal product in each industry. Capital will also distribute itself throughout the system of industries, tending, of course, in the long run, to appear in each industry in such proportions as will, apart from inequalities of risk, produce everywhere an equality of its returns. Assuming the distribution of capital to have reached a condition of equilib-

---

[1] Put in proximate and practical language, the amount of ore that can be taken profitably from a mine depends jointly on the price of the ore at the surface and the wages of labor.

rium—it being no part of our present task to follow out a theory of interest—let us try to show that labor will distribute itself over the field of industry in such a manner that exchange values will be proportionate to marginal labor costs. If labor flows from one industry to another, the total output of the first industry will decline and that of the second will increase. The change in the supplies of the respective products of these industries will alter the exchange values of these articles. Different distributions of labor among industries will give rise to different relative supplies of commodities and different exchange values. As the supply of labor in any industry increases, its marginal product decreases. If all occupations possessed the same disutility, the supply of labor would be so distributed that its marginal product would have the same exchange value in all industries. But if some occupations necessitate higher disutility costs than ordinary, the supply of labor obtainable for those industries will decrease until the exchange value of the marginal product is raised till it compensates for the superior disutility.[1] If one commodity is produced at a higher disutility cost (to the labor directly employed upon it) than another, the marginal product of labor in it will have a higher exchange value. If 6 A in one industry and 1 B in another make the marginal product of a labor-day, 6 A will exchange for 1 B, provided the disutility of labor is the same in both employments. But if it costs more disutility to produce 6 A

[1] A rise of the exchange value of the specific product of labor compensates for superior disutility by enabling the laborer to purchase things of higher esteem value with his enhanced wages. In other words, we have been explaining the familiar doctrine that wages tend to be higher in employments of higher cost. If a laborer were free to choose the precise length of his own working day, he would stop when the final disutility of the labor and the utility of the commodities purchased by the marginal increment of wages are equivalent.

than 1 B, the relative supplies of A's and B's would be
so adjusted that 6 A will exchange for more than 1 B.
Thus a superior disutility cost raises the exchange value
of a commodity, in order that this commodity may afford
a superior value product to labor.   Labor-power is a peculiar production good.   Like other production goods of
manifold productive uses, its expenditure constitutes potentiality cost; but it is unlike others in that human pain cost
is an ever-present incident to its expenditure.   The distribution of labor power among different productive uses
is not governed solely with reference to its share of value
derived from the product, but is governed in part with
reference to the pain-cost involved in the production of
the product.   A higher disutility necessitates a higher share
of exchange value.   Thus it comes to pass that this most
disposable and important of production goods will distribute itself among products in such a manner that
these products will have exchange values in proportion to
their marginal pain costs.   This result is brought about
solely by control of the relative supplies of these products,
the exchange values of which are all derived from utility
solely after the method described in the utility theory.

When we introduce the question of skill into the problem, we find that the supplies of many kinds of labor are
limited not with reference to the disutility of the tasks
performed, but are limited solely because the requisite brain-
power, ingenuity or strength are scarce.   The marginal
product of such labor is raised by the limitation of its
supply.   Thus, it is a truism that many occupations of the
lowest disutility afford very high wages, and that in the
vast majority of cases high wages are not caused by high
disutility, but by scarcity of competent persons.   Suppose
the commodity A is scarce, is of high exchange value, and
is the marginal product of a skilled labor day.   Article B

is the product of a day of the lowest kind of labor. One A may well exchange for three or four B. Yet the marginal labor cost of A is, in the typical case, even less than that of B, for the skilled laborer ordinarily suffers less pain cost per day than the unskilled. Hence, the exchange values of these products are quite out of proportion to their comparative marginal disutility costs. The existence of non-competing groups, first emphasized and named such by Cairnes, is then a fatal obstacle in the way of the adjustment of exchange values to comparative marginal costs.

8. We may now essay a partial summary of the results which have been reached up to this point. The end of the theory of value is primarily to explain exchange value. The only workable definition of this term is purchasing power. The purchasing power of a commodity is measured objectively in terms of the physical units of some other particular good, except when we are speaking of the concept of an article's *general* purchasing power. This, its purchasing power over all other commodities,[1] is measured as some kind of mean or average of all its particular purchasing powers. What mean, it is no part of our task to enquire. All goods which possess exchange value also possess that other kind of worth which we termed " esteem value." Every commodity derives its exchange value solely from its esteem value, or, speaking with precision, from its esteem values. For a commodity has a separate esteem value to each individual person who can utilize it. If society were as one man,[2] the exchange values of goods

[1] Or, as Walsh states, it may also be defined as the article's purchasing power over all goods including itself. This is not the same concept, but is one equally entitled to the name "general purchasing power." *Op. cit.,* p. 13.

[2] The meaning of this condition, it is hoped, will be apparent from the discussion in section 6.

would be but the exponents of their relative esteem values. In other words, if a physical unit of one commodity exchanged for two units of another, the reason would be merely because the first possessed twice as much esteem value to all society as a unit of the second. But the esteem value of an article is a much more definite thing than a social estimate, *i. e.,* an "average" (or typical) estimate of worth. The esteem value of a good to a person is the measure of the amount of that person's satisfaction conditioned upon the enjoyment of the good. Goods existing in superfluous abundance give satisfaction but do not condition it, and hence lack esteem value. Taking for granted the amount of an individual's income, the esteem value which a good has for him determines his price equivalent for that good.[1] The market price, or exchange value, of a good is a *resultant* from (never in any sense an average of) the individual price equivalents placed upon it by the body of individual consumers.

The exchange value of a good varies inversely with the supply of it presented to the body of consumers. The larger the supply, the lower is the price equivalent which must be reached as the marginal determining point of its market price.[2] A change of supply alters exchange value only because it changes the marginal price equivalent.[3] In the social market, the purchasing powers of all the various products over one another depends upon their relative supplies. So far as cost of production in any form exercises any degree of control over the value of a good, it can act solely by way of influencing the supply of the good. The

[1] See p. 151.   [2] See p. 151.

[3] This proposition is stated loosely as being that an increase of supply lowers value by reducing marginal utility. In many cases, exchange value is lowered by a decline of marginal utilities, but not always. See p. 152-4.

phenomenon of the apparent regulation of the exchange values of products by their entrepreneur's costs, is but a part of a large process in which cognate (or " fellow ") products adjust their relative supplies and their exchange values to one another, to the end that the common production goods entering into all of them may produce equal productive contributions or shares of exchange value per unit in all of their productive applications.[1] The relation of the pain costs of products to their exchange values is limited to one of mere proportionality.[2] The pain cost of a product may be calculated in two very distinct ways, giving total pain cost or marginal pain cost. The total pain cost of a good, consisting in all the labor and abstinence ever endured to bring it into existence, is quite an indeterminate quantity,[3] and its influence upon the exchange value of a good is very remote and irregular. The larger part of total labor cost, the part which includes the labor directly applied to commodities, plus the labor indirectly applied by being directly applied to the raw material and machinery immediately used in their production, and so on for the few nearest generations of machines, this being the part which excludes the infinitesimal bits of labor cost expended far in the past, can be shown positively not to be in proportion to their exchange values. For commodities produced at a higher expense of rents of all kinds (as opposed to wages) have exchange values out of proportion to this calculable part of their total costs.[4] We find that the control of *marginal* cost over value is closer than that of total cost. If it were not for the existence of innumerable grades and classes of skilled labor, the sup-

[1] Compare p. 160.   [2] See p. 179.

[3] Even as economic quantities go. For concept of total pain cost see p. 182.

[4] See p. 183.

plies of produced goods would be so adjusted that their exchange values would be in proportion to their respective marginal costs. But on account of skill, we must here again characterize the influence of subjective cost as remote and irregular.

In conclusion, it is true, speaking in very loose and general terms, we may say the exchange value of a good depends both upon its utility and its costliness to mankind. But it would not be proper to say that cost and utility are equal and coördinate regulators of value. Therefore, Professor Marshall's shears simile is not to be commended. The most noteworthy changes in exchange values have been produced by discoveries which reduced the labor cost of goods. But the amount of the reduction thus produced in the exchange value of a particular commodity could have only the roughest correspondence with the amount by which its relative pain cost was reduced. Also, for reasons already shown, we know that neither before or after these changes was it possible for exchange values to be in proportion to relative pain costs, whether total or marginal costs be taken. Furthermore, all alterations of exchange values produced by cost changes are effected solely by alteration of the value-determining utility itself. Utility has a much more direct and intimate relation with value in either form than cost. Value may exist without cost and cost may be expended without occasioning value. Value never exists without utility and utility (not in the sense of Smith's " use-value," but the effectual utility, the utility which measures the satisfaction conditioned by a good) never exists without value. Cost affects value solely by influencing utility itself. From this comes the all-important conclusion that whenever any of the numerous and permanent forces are active which interfere with the influence of cost, value follows the utility and not the cost.

INDEX OF AUTHORS MENTIONED.

VITA

ALBERT C. WHITAKER, the author of this dissertation, was born in Franklin, Pennsylvania, July 5, 1877. In 1890 his family moved to California, and he received his preparatory education in the High School of Los Angeles. Entering Leland Stanford Junior University in 1895, he graduated in 1899 from the department of economics with the degree of A. B. While at this institution he came under Professors H. H. Powers, E. A. Ross and F. A. Fetter. The two years following graduation were spent in the study of economics and finance in Columbia University, under Professors Richmond Mayo-Smith, Edwin R. A. Seligman, John B. Clark and Franklin H. Giddings. During his first year at Columbia, Mr. Whitaker held a Scholarship, during his second year, a Fellowship, in Economics. In his third year of graduate study, he attended lectures under Professors Adolph Wagner and Gustav Schmoller, in the University in Berlin. From 1902 to 1904 he has been an instructor in economics in Stanford University.

197